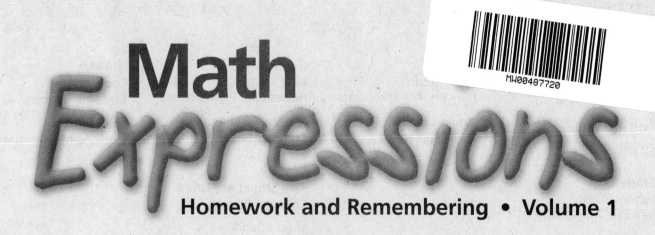

Math Expressions

Homework and Remembering • Volume 1

Developed by
The Children's Math Worlds Research Project

PROJECT DIRECTOR AND AUTHOR
Dr. Karen C. Fuson

This material is based upon work supported by the
National Science Foundation
under Grant Numbers
ESI-9816320, REC-9806020, and RED-935373.

Any opinions, findings, and conclusions, or recommendations expressed in this material
are those of the author and do not necessarily reflect the views of the National Science Foundation.

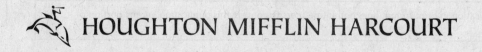

HOUGHTON MIFFLIN HARCOURT

Teacher Reviewers

Kindergarten
Patricia Stroh Sugiyama
Wilmette, Illinois

Barbara Wahle
Evanston, Illinois

Grade 1
Sandra Budson
Newton, Massachusetts

Janet Pecci
Chicago, Illinois

Megan Rees
Chicago, Illinois

Grade 2
Molly Dunn
Danvers, Massachusetts

Agnes Lesnick
Hillside, Illinois

Rita Soto
Chicago, Illinois

Grade 3
Jane Curran
Honesdale, Pennsylvania

Sandra Tucker
Chicago, Illinois

Grade 4
Sara Stoneberg Llibre
Chicago, Illinois

Sheri Roedel
Chicago, Illinois

Grade 5
Todd Atler
Chicago, Illinois

Leah Barry
Norfolk, Massachusetts

Credits

(t) © Charles Cormany/Workbook Stock/Jupiter Images, (b) Noah Strycker/Shutterstock

Ilustrative art: Robin Boyer/Deborah Wolfe, LTD; Geoff Smith, Tim Johnson
Technical art: Nesbitt Graphics, Inc.
Photos: Nesbitt Graphics, Inc.

ISBN: 978-0-547-06675-2

14 15 16 1689 16 15 14 13
4500407880   C D E F G

Name _____

Homework

Solve the story problems.   **Show your work.**

1. Spencer saw 8 frogs in the pond. Then he saw 5 more. How many frogs did Spencer see altogether?

   ▢ _____
        label

frog

2. Beth has 5 red marbles and some blue marbles. Altogether she has 14 marbles. How many of the marbles are blue?

   ▢ _____
        label

marbles

3. Felix has 5 stamps from Mexico. The rest are from Canada. He has 8 stamps altogether. How many stamps are from Canada?

   ▢ _____
        label

stamp

4. Gary had 7 books. His mother gave him 3 more books. How many books does Gary have now?

   ▢ _____
        label

book

5. **On the Back** Write your own story problem. Then show how to solve it.

Introduce Stories and Drawings **1**

Name _____

_____

_____

_____

_____

_____

_____

_____

Introduce Stories and Drawings

Homework

Name _____

Solve the story problems.   **Show your work.**

---

1. There were 15 lights on. Then some of the lights burned out. Now there are 6 lights on. How many lights burned out?

light

☐ _____
label

---

2. Kari scored 7 points at soccer practice. Shona scored 3. How many more points did Kari score than Shona?

soccer ball

☐ _____
label

---

3. There are 4 screwdrivers and some hammers in a toolbox. Altogether there are 9 tools. How many hammers are there?

tools

☐ _____
label

---

4. Obi picked 14 cucumbers. Pam picked 8. How many more cucumbers would Pam have to pick to have as many as Obi?

cucumber

☐ _____
label

---

5. Show a Proof Drawing Choose one of the problems on this page. Show a Proof Drawing for the problem.

Remembering

Solve the story problems.   **Show your work.**

1. Andy has 9 toys. Andy gave Yori 4 toys.
   How many toys does Andy have left?

   ☐ _____
        label

toy

2. Tracy has 7 green marbles and some
   yellow marbles. Altogether she has 10
   marbles. How many of them are yellow?

   ☐ _____
        label

marbles

3. Imala has 5 balls. John has 2. How many
   balls do they have altogether?

   ☐ _____
        label

ball

4. There are 3 boys and some girls on the
   train. There are 7 children on the train.
   How many girls are on the train?

   ☐ _____
        label

train

5. **Explain Your Thinking** On a separate piece of
   paper, explain all the steps you took to solve
   problem 4.

Homework

Name _____

Add or subtract.

1. 7 + 1 = ☐   5 − 0 = ☐   0 + 1 = ☐

2. 3 + 0 = ☐   9 − 1 = ☐   6 + 1 = ☐

3. 0 + 7 = ☐   2 − 0 = ☐   4 + 1 = ☐

4. 4 + 1 = ☐   3 − 1 = ☐   6 + 0 = ☐

5. 9 + 0 = ☐   5 − 1 = ☐   9 + 1 = ☐

6. 1 + 8 = ☐   2 − 1 = ☐   10 − 0 = ☐

7. 1 + 3 = ☐   4 − 0 = ☐   8 − 0 = ☐

8. 0 + 5 = ☐   6 − 0 = ☐   3 + 1 = ☐

9. 5 + 1 = ☐   7 − 1 = ☐   6 − 1 = ☐

10. 0 + 4 = ☐   8 − 0 = ☐   1 − 1 = ☐

 11. **On the Back** What happens when you add 0 to a number? Draw a picture to explain.

Name

Add or Subtract 0 or I

Name _____

Homework

Solve the story problems. **Show your work.**

---

1. There were 12 clean glasses in the dish rack. Matt put some of them away. Now there are 5 glasses left in the rack. How many glasses did Matt put away?

glasses

[ ] _____
label

---

2. There are 2 flowers in a red vase and some flowers in a white vase. There are 8 flowers altogether. How many flowers are in the white vase?

flowers

[ ] _____
label

---

3. Carlos took 10 pictures with his camera. Jane took 6 pictures. How many more pictures must Jane take in order to have as many as Carlos?

camera

[ ] _____
label

---

4. Jung Mee has 9 tomatoes growing in her garden. She has 8 tomatoes in the kitchen. How many tomatoes does Jung Mee have in total?

tomato

[ ] _____
label

Remembering

Solve the story problems.   **Show your work.**

1. Mary spent $3 at the toy store. Jamal spent
   $6 more than Mary. How many dollars did
   Jamal spend at the toy store?

toy

   [ ] _____
        label

2. Aaron bought 5 hats at the store. Lucia
   bought 8 hats. How many more hats must
   Aaron buy to have as many as Lucia?

hat

   [ ] _____
        label

Add or subtract 0 or 1.

3. $4 + 1 =$ [ ] $9 - 1 =$ [ ] $0 + 7 =$ [ ]

4. $9 + 1 =$ [ ] $6 - 0 =$ [ ] $2 + 0 =$ [ ]

5. $1 + 3 =$ [ ] $6 - 1 =$ [ ] $9 + 0 =$ [ ]

6. $0 + 5 =$ [ ] $8 - 0 =$ [ ] $6 + 1 =$ [ ]

7. $7 + 1 =$ [ ] $7 - 1 =$ [ ] $1 + 5 =$ [ ]

8. $0 + 4 =$ [ ] $1 - 1 =$ [ ] $1 + 8 =$ [ ]

1. What teen numbers are shown here?

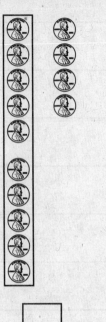
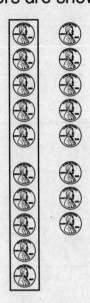
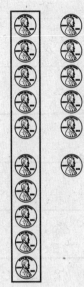

☐   ☐   ☐

$10 + 6 =$ _____

$10 + 2 =$ _____

$10 + 4 =$ _____

$10 + 1 =$ _____

$10 + 3 =$ _____

$10 + 5 =$ _____

$10 + 8 =$ _____

$10 + 7 =$ _____

$10 + 9 =$ _____

2. Ring the pennies needed to make each teen number.

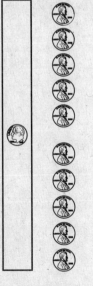

17   12   15

$12 = 10 +$ _____

$16 = 10 +$ _____

$18 = 10 +$ _____

$11 = 10 +$ _____

$17 = 10 +$ _____

$14 = 10 +$ _____

$13 = 10 +$ _____

$15 = 10 +$ _____

$19 = 10 +$ _____

3. On the Back Write and solve a story problem about pennies.

Name _____

_____

_____

_____

_____

_____

_____

_____

_____

Teens, Tens, and Dimes

Homework

Count the rabbits in the garden. Then write the partners of 10.

1.

10 = ___ + ___   10 = ___ + ___   10 = ___ + ___

2.

10 = ___ + ___   10 = ___ + ___   10 = ___ + ___

3.

10 = ___ + ___   10 = ___ + ___   10 = ___ + ___

4. Write the partners of 10 that are the same but are switched.

__1__ + __9__ = __9__ + __1__   ___ + ___ = ___ + ___

___ + ___ = ___ + ___   ___ + ___ = ___ + ___

Name _____

Remembering

Solve the story problems.   **Show your work.**

---

1. Sally had 9 tomatoes. She and her friends
ate 4. How many tomatoes are left?

tomato

☐ _____
     label

---

2. On Jerome's desk, 6 folders are open.
The rest are closed. There are 9 folders
on Jerome's desk. How many folders on
his desk are closed?

folder

☐ _____
     label

What teen numbers are shown here?

3.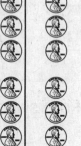

$19 = 10 + \underline{\hphantom{xx}}$

$12 = 10 + \underline{\hphantom{xx}}$

$14 = 10 + \underline{\hphantom{xx}}$

$18 = 10 + \underline{\hphantom{xx}}$

$11 = 10 + \underline{\hphantom{xx}}$

$15 = 10 + \underline{\hphantom{xx}}$

$17 = 10 + \underline{\hphantom{xx}}$

$13 = 10 + \underline{\hphantom{xx}}$

$16 = 10 + \underline{\hphantom{xx}}$

Homework

Write the number partners and the total for the picture.

1.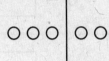

Number Partners

_____ and _____

Total _____

2.

Number Partners

_____ and _____

Total _____

3. ○○○○
○○○○

Number Partners

_____ and _____

Total _____

4.

○○○ | ○○

Number Partners

_____ and _____

Total _____

5. ○○○○○
○○○○

Number Partners

_____ and _____

Total _____

6. ○○ | ○○
○ | ○○

Number Partners

_____ and _____

Total _____

7. **Create Your Own** Draw your own picture.

Write the number partners and total for your picture.

Number Partners

_____ and _____

Total _____

Targeted Practice

Watch the signs!

Add or subtract.

1. $4 + 1 =$ ☐ $1 - 1 =$ ☐ $5 - 1 =$ ☐

2. $6 + 1 =$ ☐ $8 - 0 =$ ☐ $3 - 1 =$ ☐

3. $0 + 1 =$ ☐ $8 - 1 =$ ☐ $2 - 0 =$ ☐

4. $0 + 10 =$ ☐ $1 - 0 =$ ☐ $9 - 1 =$ ☐

5. $8 + 1 =$ ☐ $4 - 1 =$ ☐ $5 - 0 =$ ☐

6. $1 + 0 =$ ☐ $10 - 1 =$ ☐ $7 - 0 =$ ☐

7. $5 + 1 =$ ☐ $9 - 0 =$ ☐ $1 + 7 =$ ☐

8. $6 + 0 =$ ☐ $10 - 0 =$ ☐ $9 - 0 =$ ☐

9. **Critical Thinking** How are adding 0 and subtracting 0 the same?

_____

_____

Name _____

Homework

Complete the Partner Houses.

1.

8
+	+
+	+
+	+
+	

2
| + | |

5
| + | + |
| + | + |

2.

3
| + | + |

6
+	+
+	+
+	

10
+	+
+	+
+	+
+	+
+	

3.

7
+	+
+	+
+	+

9
+	+
+	+
+	+
+	+

4
| + | + |
| + | |

4. Which Partner Houses have doubles?

_____

Remembering

Count the rabbits in the garden. Then write
the partners of 10. Then switch the partners.

1.    **2.**    **3.**

10 = ___ + ___   10 = ___ + ___   10 = ___ + ___

10 = ___ + ___   10 = ___ + ___   10 = ___ + ___

What teen numbers are shown here?

4.    **5.**    **6.** 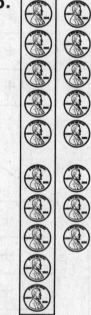   **7.**

Name _____

Homework

$$6 + 3 = \boxed{9}$$

... **Already 6** 7 8 9	I pretend I already counted 6. So **6**, <u>7</u>, <u>8</u>, <u>9</u>.

• • • **Already 6** 7 8 9	8 9 **Already 6** 7 

Count on to find the total.

1. 5 + 4 = ☐   4 + 7 = ☐   7 + 2 = ☐

2. 4 + 3 = ☐   2 + 6 = ☐   5 + 2 = ☐

3. 7 + 5 = ☐   5 + 7 = ☐   9 + 6 = ☐

4. 4 + 6 = ☐   3 + 8 = ☐   8 + 6 = ☐

5. 5 + 8 = ☐   7 + 9 = ☐   9 + 4 = ☐

6. 5 + 9 = ☐   2 + 6 = ☐   4 + 6 = ☐

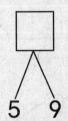   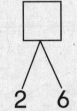   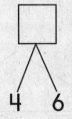

7. Write About It Explain how you can find the total for
5 + 9. What is the total?

_____

_____

Name _____

Targeted Practice

Complete the Partner Houses.

1.

```
        10
    +   |   +
    +   |   +
    +   |   +
    +   |   +
    +   | ▓▓▓
```

```
        9
    +   |   +
    +   |   +
    +   |   +
    +   |   +
```

```
        8
    +   |   +
    +   |   +
    +   |   +
    +   | ▓▓▓
```

2.

```
        7
    +   |   +
    +   |   +
    +   |   +
```

```
        6
    +   |   +
    +   |   +
    +   | ▓▓▓
```

```
        5
    +   |   +
    +   |   +
```

3.

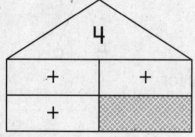

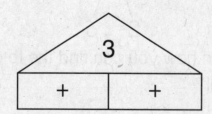

Count On to Find the Total

Stop when
I hear 8

Already **5** 6 7 8

$$5 + \boxed{3} = 8$$

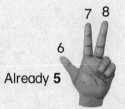

Already **5**

3 more to make 8

Stop when
I hear 8

I took 5 away   6 7 8

3 more to make 8

$$8 - 5 = \boxed{3}$$

Count on to find the partner.

1. $7 + \boxed{} = 9$ $9 - 6 = \boxed{}$ $3 + \boxed{} = 8$

2. $5 + \boxed{} = 8$ $10 - 7 = \boxed{}$ $3 + \boxed{} = 9$

3. $7 + \boxed{} = 10$ $10 - 4 = \boxed{}$ $7 + \boxed{} = 11$

4. $6 + \boxed{} = 8$ $8 - 3 = \boxed{}$ $6 + \boxed{} = 9$

5. $2 + \boxed{} = 9$ $8 - 6 = \boxed{}$ $11 - 7 = \boxed{}$

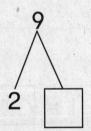

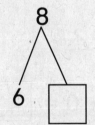

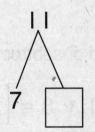

6. **Explain Your Thinking** Explain how you found the

answer for $11 - 7 = \boxed{}$.

_____

_____

Remembering

Complete the Partner Houses.

1.

```
      9                   6                   8
  +   |   +          +   |   +          +   |   +
  +   |   +          +   |   +          +   |   +
  +   |   +          +   |   +          +   |   +
  +   |   +          +   |░░░         +   |░░░
```

Solve the story problem.　　　　　　　　　**Show your work.**

_____

2. Rachel had 9 toy cars. She gave 7 toy
cars to her friends. How many toy cars
does Rachel have now?

toy car

☐ _____
　　label

_____

Add or subtract 0 or 1.

3. 1 + 8 = ☐　　　　2 − 0 = ☐　　　　8 + 1 = ☐

4. 1 + 3 = ☐　　　　5 − 1 = ☐　　　　0 + 1 = ☐

5. 1 + 9 = ☐　　　　6 − 1 = ☐　　　　9 − 1 = ☐

6. 0 + 5 = ☐　　　　8 − 0 = ☐　　　　6 − 0 = ☐

　　　　　　Count On to Find the Partner

Name _____

Homework

Make a ten or count on to find the total.

1. $4 + 8 =$ ☐ $4 + 6 =$ ☐ $5 + 7 =$ ☐

2. $5 + 6 =$ ☐ $5 + 8 =$ ☐ $9 + 3 =$ ☐

3. $3 + 8 =$ ☐ $7 + 4 =$ ☐ $9 + 5 =$ ☐

4. $7 + 7 =$ ☐ $2 + 8 =$ ☐ $4 + 9 =$ ☐

5. $6 + 9 =$ ☐ $5 + 9 =$ ☐ $6 + 8 =$ ☐

6. $6 + 4 =$ ☐ $8 + 9 =$ ☐ $6 + 7 =$ ☐

7. $8 + 2 =$ ☐ $8 + 3 =$ ☐ $9 + 9 =$ ☐

8. $7 + 8 =$ ☐ $8 + 4 =$ ☐ $9 + 2 =$ ☐

9. $8 + 6 =$ ☐ $7 + 9 =$ ☐ $5 + 5 =$ ☐

10. **Explain Your Thinking** Choose one equation above.
Explain how you found the total.

_____

_____

Name _____

Targeted Practice

$$6 + 3 = \boxed{9}$$

6

Already **6** • • • 7 8 9

6

Already **6**   • • •   7 8 9

7 8 9

Already **6**

Count on to find the total.

1. $8 + 7 = \boxed{}$ $2 + 9 = \boxed{}$ $7 + 5 = \boxed{}$

2. $5 + 6 = \boxed{}$ $3 + 9 = \boxed{}$ $6 + 9 = \boxed{}$

3. $4 + 8 = \boxed{}$ $4 + 7 = \boxed{}$ $6 + 6 = \boxed{}$

4. $7 + 4 = \boxed{}$ $3 + 8 = \boxed{}$ $8 + 4 = \boxed{}$

5. $9 + 5 = \boxed{}$ $4 + 9 = \boxed{}$ $8 + 5 = \boxed{}$

6. $8 + 6 = \boxed{}$ $7 + 7 = \boxed{}$ $4 + 8 = \boxed{}$

7. $9 + 9 = \boxed{}$ $6 + 5 = \boxed{}$ $8 + 8 = \boxed{}$

8. **Critical Thinking** How can you use counting on to solve this equation? $7 + 5 = \boxed{}$

_____

_____

Homework

Make a ten or count on to find the total.

1. 3 + 8 = ☐   4 + 8 = ☐   4 + 9 = ☐

2. 8 + 6 = ☐   9 + 5 = ☐   8 + 5 = ☐

3. 6 + 7 = ☐   7 + 7 = ☐   7 + 5 = ☐

4. 2 + 9 = ☐   5 + 7 = ☐   9 + 2 = ☐

5. 3 + 9 = ☐   8 + 9 = ☐   4 + 7 = ☐

6. 9 + 8 = ☐   7 + 6 = ☐   5 + 9 = ☐

7. 6 + 9 = ☐   6 + 6 = ☐   5 + 6 = ☐

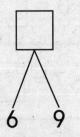   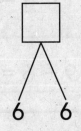   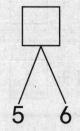

8. **Critical Thinking** Explain how to make a ten to find 8 + 6.

_____

_____

Name _____

Remembering

Complete each Partner House.

1.

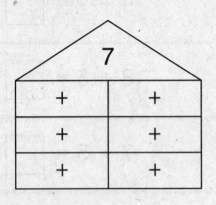

Count on to find the partner.

2. $6 +$ ☐ $= 10$ $10 - 7 =$ ☐ $3 +$ ☐ $= 6$

3. $3 +$ ☐ $= 12$ $10 - 5 =$ ☐ $4 +$ ☐ $= 7$

4. $4 +$ ☐ $= 9$ $13 - 7 =$ ☐ $9 +$ ☐ $= 14$

5. $6 +$ ☐ $= 8$ $11 - 4 =$ ☐ $8 - 3 =$ ☐

6. $8 +$ ☐ $= 13$ $9 - 6 =$ ☐ $11 - 7 =$ ☐

7. $7 +$ ☐ $= 9$ $10 - 8 =$ ☐ $11 - 9 =$ ☐

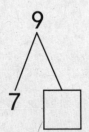

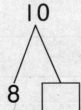

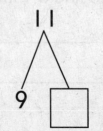

Make a Ten with Penny Strips and Fingers

Homework

Make a ten or count on to find the total.

1. 3 + 8 = ☐   4 + 8 = ☐   4 + 9 = ☐

2. 8 + 6 = ☐   9 + 5 = ☐   8 + 5 = ☐

3. 6 + 7 = ☐   7 + 7 = ☐   7 + 5 = ☐

4. 7 + 4 = ☐   8 + 9 = ☐   4 + 7 = ☐

5. 9 + 8 = ☐   7 + 6 = ☐   5 + 9 = ☐

6. 3 + 9 = ☐   6 + 5 = ☐   5 + 8 = ☐

7. 6 + 9 = ☐   6 + 6 = ☐   5 + 6 = ☐

8. **Critical Thinking** How you can use
the Make a Ten strategy to solve
8 + ☐ = 14?

_____

_____

Targeted Practice

$$8 - 5 = \boxed{3}$$

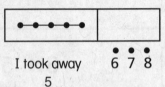

I took away
5

6 7 8

3 more to make 8

or

I took away
5

3 more to make 8

Count on to find the partner.

1. $8 - 4 = \boxed{}$ $9 - 6 = \boxed{}$ $10 - 8 = \boxed{}$

2. $7 - 5 = \boxed{}$ $10 - 4 = \boxed{}$ $6 - 3 = \boxed{}$

3. $9 - 3 = \boxed{}$ $8 - 5 = \boxed{}$ $6 - 5 = \boxed{}$

4. $3 - 2 = \boxed{}$ $8 - 6 = \boxed{}$ $10 - 2 = \boxed{}$

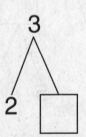

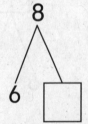

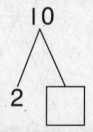

5. The yard sale records got wet.
Some numbers are missing. Fill in
the missing numbers.

Item	Number Sold Each Day		
	Saturday	Sunday	Total
Birdhouse	1	6	
Potholder	4		9
Picture Frame	2		10

Homework

1. Complete the Math Mountains and equations.

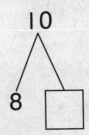

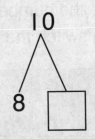

$8 + 2 = \boxed{}$

$8 + \boxed{} = 10$

$10 - 8 = \boxed{}$

---

2. Create and Solve Write and solve a story problem
for one of the equations above.

_____

_____

_____

_____

---

3. Draw a Picture and Explain Draw two different
Math Mountains with a total of 12. Explain why you
can make two different Math Mountains.

_____

_____

_____

_____

Name _____

Remembering

Count the rabbits in the garden.
Write the numbers hidden inside the 10.
Then switch the partners.

1.

10 = ___ + ___   10 = ___ + ___   10 = ___ + ___

10 = ___ + ___   10 = ___ + ___   10 = ___ + ___

Solve the story problems.   **Show your work.**

2. James had 11 rose bushes. He planted 6
in the back yard and the rest in the front
yard. How many rose bushes did he plant
in the front yard?

rose bush

☐ _____
       label

3. Josh had 12 daisies in his hand. He put
some in a vase. He has 3 left in his hand.
How many daisies did he put in the vase?

daisies

☐ _____
       label

Relate Addition and Subtraction

Name _____

Homework

$$8 + \boxed{6} = 14 \quad \text{or} \quad 14 - 8 = \boxed{6}$$

Already **8**   9̇ 10 11 12 13 14

or   **8**   9̇ 10 + 4 more

                    6

or   **8**   + 2 + 4 = 14

or   **8**   10 + 4

Already **8**

2 more to
10

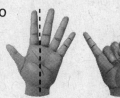

4 more to
14

Find the partner.

1. $5 + \boxed{} = 12$ $15 - 8 = \boxed{}$ $8 + \boxed{} = 16$

2. $7 + \boxed{} = 16$ $13 - 4 = \boxed{}$ $9 + \boxed{} = 12$

3. $3 + \boxed{} = 12$ $11 - 2 = \boxed{}$ $7 + \boxed{} = 13$

4. $9 + \boxed{} = 15$ $14 - 8 = \boxed{}$ $17 - 9 = \boxed{}$

5. $8 + \boxed{} = 12$ $16 - 8 = \boxed{}$ $16 - 7 = \boxed{}$

6. $5 + \boxed{} = 13$ $18 - 9 = \boxed{}$ $12 - 7 = \boxed{}$

7. $4 + \boxed{} = 12$ $11 - 4 = \boxed{}$ $12 - 9 = \boxed{}$

8. **Explain Your Thinking** Choose one equation above.
   Explain how you can make a ten to find the partner.

_____

Targeted Practice

$$8 + 6 = \boxed{14}$$

Already **8** $\overset{\bullet}{9}\ \overset{\bullet}{10}\ \overset{\bullet}{11}\ \overset{\bullet}{12}\ \overset{\bullet}{13}\ \overset{\bullet}{14}$

or **8** $\overset{\bullet}{9}\ \overset{\bullet}{10}$ + 4 more

or **8** $+ \overset{6}{2} + 4 = 14$

or **8** $10 + 4 = 14$

Already **8**

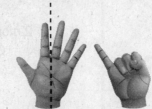

6 gives 2 to 8 to make 10
4 left in 6, so **10 + 4 = 14**

Think 8 + 6
$8 + 2 + 4 = 14$
10

Make a ten or count on to find the total.

1. $6 + 9 = \square$ $6 + 6 = \square$ $3 + 8 = \square$

2. $6 + 5 = \square$ $5 + 8 = \square$ $6 + 7 = \square$

3. $9 + 8 = \square$ $7 + 6 = \square$ $7 + 4 = \square$

4. $8 + 9 = \square$ $4 + 7 = \square$ $3 + 9 = \square$

5. $2 + 9 = \square$ $5 + 7 = \square$ $8 + 5 = \square$

6. $7 + 7 = \square$ $7 + 5 = \square$ $9 + 2 = \square$

7. $8 + 6 = \square$ $9 + 5 = \square$ $5 + 6 = \square$

8. $4 + 8 = \square$ $4 + 9 = \square$ $5 + 9 = \square$

Unknown Partners and Teen Totals

Write the partner.

1. $6 + \boxed{} = 15$ $17 - 8 = \boxed{}$ $3 + \boxed{} = 11$

2. $9 + \boxed{} = 17$ $12 - 6 = \boxed{}$ $9 + \boxed{} = 12$

3. $5 + \boxed{} = 11$ $12 - 4 = \boxed{}$ $7 + \boxed{} = 12$

4. $8 + \boxed{} = 13$ $15 - 7 = \boxed{}$ $5 + \boxed{} = 14$

5. $7 + \boxed{} = 11$ $15 - 8 = \boxed{}$ $13 - 7 = \boxed{}$

6. $9 + \boxed{} = 14$ $13 - 5 = \boxed{}$ $11 - 6 = \boxed{}$

7. $5 + \boxed{} = 12$ $12 - 3 = \boxed{}$ $11 - 2 = \boxed{}$

8. $8 + \boxed{} = 13$ $15 - 9 = \boxed{}$ $13 - 6 = \boxed{}$

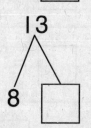   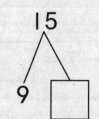   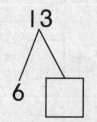

9. **Critical Thinking** Explain how the math drawing can help you solve $8 + \boxed{} = 14$.

Already **8** $\overset{\cdots\ \mid\ \cdots\cdot}{10\ +\ 4}\ =\ 14$

_____

_____

Name _____

Remembering

Solve the story problem.   **Show your work.**

1. Ellen has 12 books in her bag.
   She put 6 of the books on the table.
   How many books are in her bag now?

   book

   [ ] _____
          label

Complete the Partner Houses.

2.
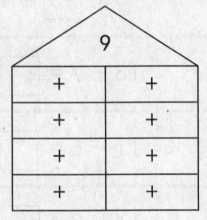

Write the partner.

3. 5 + [ ] = 11   13 − 9 = [ ]   5 + [ ] = 13

4. 9 + [ ] = 14   12 − 7 = [ ]   8 + [ ] = 14

5. 8 + [ ] = 12   15 − 9 = [ ]   16 − 8 = [ ]

6. 7 + [ ] = 13   17 − 8 = [ ]   11 − 4 = [ ]

Relate Addition and Subtraction–Teen Totals

Count on to find the total or partner.

Circle the addends to see how the number line works for addition.

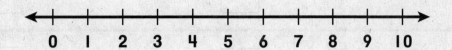

1. 5 + 5 = ☐

2. 8 − 3 = ☐

3. 7 + 2 = ☐

4. 5 − 2 = ☐

5. 4 + 1 = ☐

6. 7 − 3 = ☐

7. 6 − 2 = ☐

8. 5 + 4 = ☐

9. 9 − 4 = ☐

10. 6 + 2 = ☐

10. **Write About It** Explain how you would use a number line to solve 3 + 4 = ☐ .

_____

_____

_____

Targeted Practice

Count on to find the total.

1. $7 + 5 = \boxed{}$ $3 + 7 = \boxed{}$ $5 + 4 = \boxed{}$

2. $9 + 4 = \boxed{}$ $2 + 9 = \boxed{}$ $8 + 5 = \boxed{}$

3. $8 + 6 = \boxed{}$ $4 + 6 = \boxed{}$ $3 + 6 = \boxed{}$

4. $7 + 3 = \boxed{}$ $8 + 4 = \boxed{}$ $8 + 3 = \boxed{}$

5. $6 + 9 = \boxed{}$ $4 + 8 = \boxed{}$ $5 + 6 = \boxed{}$

6. $7 + 8 = \boxed{}$ $7 + 7 = \boxed{}$ $9 + 3 = \boxed{}$

7. $4 + 5 = \boxed{}$ $6 + 8 = \boxed{}$ $7 + 9 = \boxed{}$

Solve the story problem.   **Show your work.**

8. Gina has 5 crayons. Peter has 6 crayons. How many crayons do they have altogether?

$\boxed{}$ _____
      label

crayon

Homework

$$9 + 4 = \boxed{13} \qquad\qquad 13 - 9 = \boxed{4}$$

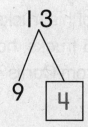

$$\boxed{13}$$

$$9$$
$$+ 4$$
$$\overline{13}$$

9   4

I find the total.

$$13$$

9   $\boxed{4}$

$$13$$
$$- 9$$
$$\overline{4}$$

I find a partner.

Find the total or partner.

1.
$$\begin{array}{r} 5 \\ + 6 \\ \hline \end{array} \qquad \begin{array}{r} 9 \\ + 8 \\ \hline \end{array} \qquad \begin{array}{r} 8 \\ + 3 \\ \hline \end{array} \qquad \begin{array}{r} 9 \\ + 4 \\ \hline \end{array} \qquad \begin{array}{r} 6 \\ + 6 \\ \hline \end{array} \qquad \begin{array}{r} 8 \\ + 6 \\ \hline \end{array}$$

2.
$$\begin{array}{r} 11 \\ - 9 \\ \hline \end{array} \qquad \begin{array}{r} 14 \\ - 6 \\ \hline \end{array} \qquad \begin{array}{r} 11 \\ - 4 \\ \hline \end{array} \qquad \begin{array}{r} 13 \\ - 5 \\ \hline \end{array} \qquad \begin{array}{r} 12 \\ - 3 \\ \hline \end{array} \qquad \begin{array}{r} 16 \\ - 9 \\ \hline \end{array}$$

3.
$$\begin{array}{r} 16 \\ - 8 \\ \hline \end{array} \qquad \begin{array}{r} 15 \\ - 7 \\ \hline \end{array} \qquad \begin{array}{r} 12 \\ - 5 \\ \hline \end{array} \qquad \begin{array}{r} 11 \\ - 2 \\ \hline \end{array} \qquad \begin{array}{r} 17 \\ - 9 \\ \hline \end{array} \qquad \begin{array}{r} 16 \\ - 7 \\ \hline \end{array}$$

4. Draw a Math Mountain to solve for $16 - 7 = \boxed{}$.

Name _____

Remembering

Solve the story problem.   **Show your work.**

1. Yesterday John bought 8 trucks. Today Curtis gave some of his trucks to John. If John now has 15 trucks, how many trucks did he get from Curtis?

   ☐ _____ label

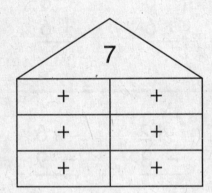
truck

Complete the Partner Houses.

2.

House with 7:
+	+
+	+
+	+

House with 6:
+	+
+	+
+	▨

House with 9:
+	+
+	+
+	+
+	+

Make a ten or count on to find the total or partner.

3. $9 + \boxed{} = 13$ $11 - 2 = \boxed{}$ $7 + 4 = \boxed{}$

4. $2 + \boxed{} = 11$ $11 - 6 = \boxed{}$ $9 + 8 = \boxed{}$

5. $5 + \boxed{} = 14$ $13 - 6 = \boxed{}$ $7 + 8 = \boxed{}$

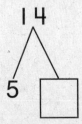

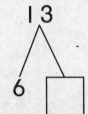

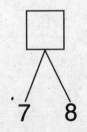

Equations and Equation Chains

Homework

Find the total or the partner. Draw squiggles under the partners.

1. 5 + 9 = ☐   5 + ☐ = 14   14 − 5 = ☐

2. 9 + 6 = ☐   9 + ☐ = 15   15 − 9 = ☐

3. 4 + 7 = ☐   4 + ☐ = 11   11 − 4 = ☐

4. 6 + 5 = ☐   6 + ☐ = 11   11 − 6 = ☐

5. 5 + 7 = ☐   5 + ☐ = 12   12 − 5 = ☐

6. 8 + 6 = ☐   8 + ☐ = 14   14 − 8 = ☐

7. 3 + 9 = ☐   3 + ☐ = 12   12 − 3 = ☐

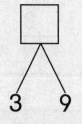   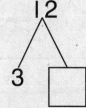   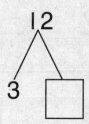

8. **Write Your Own** Write an equation to show that an
unknown number is added to 4 and the total is 13.
Write and solve a story problem that uses your equation.

_____

_____

_____

Targeted Practice

$$9 + 4 = \boxed{13}$$

$\boxed{13}$

$$\begin{array}{r} 9 \\ + 4 \\ \hline 13 \end{array}$$

9   4

$$13 - 9 = \boxed{4}$$

13

9    $\boxed{4}$

$$\begin{array}{r} 13 \\ - 9 \\ \hline 4 \end{array}$$

Add or subtract.

1.
$$\begin{array}{r} 5 \\ + 6 \\ \hline \end{array}$$
$$\begin{array}{r} 9 \\ + 3 \\ \hline \end{array}$$
$$\begin{array}{r} 8 \\ + 3 \\ \hline \end{array}$$
$$\begin{array}{r} 2 \\ + 9 \\ \hline \end{array}$$
$$\begin{array}{r} 6 \\ + 6 \\ \hline \end{array}$$
$$\begin{array}{r} 8 \\ + 6 \\ \hline \end{array}$$

2.
$$\begin{array}{r} 9 \\ + 6 \\ \hline \end{array}$$
$$\begin{array}{r} 4 \\ + 8 \\ \hline \end{array}$$
$$\begin{array}{r} 3 \\ + 9 \\ \hline \end{array}$$
$$\begin{array}{r} 7 \\ + 5 \\ \hline \end{array}$$
$$\begin{array}{r} 8 \\ + 7 \\ \hline \end{array}$$
$$\begin{array}{r} 7 \\ + 7 \\ \hline \end{array}$$

3.
$$\begin{array}{r} 17 \\ - 9 \\ \hline \end{array}$$
$$\begin{array}{r} 14 \\ - 6 \\ \hline \end{array}$$
$$\begin{array}{r} 16 \\ - 7 \\ \hline \end{array}$$
$$\begin{array}{r} 15 \\ - 8 \\ \hline \end{array}$$
$$\begin{array}{r} 11 \\ - 6 \\ \hline \end{array}$$
$$\begin{array}{r} 14 \\ - 8 \\ \hline \end{array}$$

4.
$$\begin{array}{r} 15 \\ - 9 \\ \hline \end{array}$$
$$\begin{array}{r} 14 \\ - 7 \\ \hline \end{array}$$
$$\begin{array}{r} 15 \\ - 7 \\ \hline \end{array}$$
$$\begin{array}{r} 12 \\ - 7 \\ \hline \end{array}$$
$$\begin{array}{r} 17 \\ - 8 \\ \hline \end{array}$$
$$\begin{array}{r} 13 \\ - 7 \\ \hline \end{array}$$

5.
$$\begin{array}{r} 18 \\ - 9 \\ \hline \end{array}$$
$$\begin{array}{r} 7 \\ + 6 \\ \hline \end{array}$$
$$\begin{array}{r} 16 \\ - 9 \\ \hline \end{array}$$
$$\begin{array}{r} 8 \\ + 9 \\ \hline \end{array}$$
$$\begin{array}{r} 5 \\ + 8 \\ \hline \end{array}$$
$$\begin{array}{r} 14 \\ - 5 \\ \hline \end{array}$$

Equations from Math Mountains

Homework

Name _____

$9 + 4 = \boxed{13}$ $\qquad\qquad$ $13 - 9 = \boxed{4}$

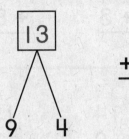

$$\begin{array}{r} 9 \\ + 4 \\ \hline 13 \end{array}$$

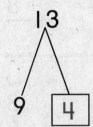

$$\begin{array}{r} 13 \\ - 9 \\ \hline 4 \end{array}$$

Write the partner or total.

1. $\begin{array}{r} 9 \\ + 3 \\ \hline \end{array}$ $\quad$ $\begin{array}{r} 5 \\ + 6 \\ \hline \end{array}$ $\quad$ $\begin{array}{r} 7 \\ + 8 \\ \hline \end{array}$ $\quad$ $\begin{array}{r} 5 \\ + 8 \\ \hline \end{array}$ $\quad$ $\begin{array}{r} 4 \\ + 8 \\ \hline \end{array}$ $\quad$ $\begin{array}{r} 7 \\ + 4 \\ \hline \end{array}$

---

2. $\begin{array}{r} 5 \\ + 9 \\ \hline \end{array}$ $\quad$ $\begin{array}{r} 9 \\ + 6 \\ \hline \end{array}$ $\quad$ $\begin{array}{r} 8 \\ + 6 \\ \hline \end{array}$ $\quad$ $\begin{array}{r} 6 \\ + 9 \\ \hline \end{array}$ $\quad$ $\begin{array}{r} 9 \\ + 7 \\ \hline \end{array}$ $\quad$ $\begin{array}{r} 8 \\ + 9 \\ \hline \end{array}$

---

3. $\begin{array}{r} 15 \\ - 9 \\ \hline \end{array}$ $\quad$ $\begin{array}{r} 11 \\ - 8 \\ \hline \end{array}$ $\quad$ $\begin{array}{r} 13 \\ - 4 \\ \hline \end{array}$ $\quad$ $\begin{array}{r} 14 \\ - 5 \\ \hline \end{array}$ $\quad$ $\begin{array}{r} 11 \\ - 3 \\ \hline \end{array}$ $\quad$ $\begin{array}{r} 11 \\ - 6 \\ \hline \end{array}$

---

4. Create Your Own Write and solve a story problem
for this equation, $8 + \boxed{} = 12$.

_____

_____

_____

Remembering

Add or subtract.

1. $\begin{array}{r} 8 \\ + 3 \\ \hline \end{array}$ $\begin{array}{r} 7 \\ + 5 \\ \hline \end{array}$ $\begin{array}{r} 4 \\ + 8 \\ \hline \end{array}$ $\begin{array}{r} 9 \\ + 9 \\ \hline \end{array}$ $\begin{array}{r} 9 \\ + 3 \\ \hline \end{array}$ $\begin{array}{r} 6 \\ + 8 \\ \hline \end{array}$

2. $\begin{array}{r} 4 \\ + 7 \\ \hline \end{array}$ $\begin{array}{r} 7 \\ + 6 \\ \hline \end{array}$ $\begin{array}{r} 8 \\ + 8 \\ \hline \end{array}$ $\begin{array}{r} 13 \\ - 4 \\ \hline \end{array}$ $\begin{array}{r} 14 \\ - 9 \\ \hline \end{array}$ $\begin{array}{r} 15 \\ - 7 \\ \hline \end{array}$

3. $\begin{array}{r} 15 \\ - 8 \\ \hline \end{array}$ $\begin{array}{r} 14 \\ - 7 \\ \hline \end{array}$ $\begin{array}{r} 11 \\ - 5 \\ \hline \end{array}$ $\begin{array}{r} 11 \\ - 2 \\ \hline \end{array}$ $\begin{array}{r} 16 \\ - 9 \\ \hline \end{array}$ $\begin{array}{r} 18 \\ - 9 \\ \hline \end{array}$

Write all of the equations for the 13, 5, 8 Math Mountain.
Draw squiggles under the partners.

4. $\underline{5 + 8 = 13}$  $\underline{13 = 5 + 8}$

    _____      _____

    _____      _____

    _____   _____

Name _____

Homework

Compare. Write < or >.

1. 4 ◯ 8   2. 10 ◯ 6   3. 9 ◯ 12

4. 15 ◯ 17   5. 14 ◯ 13   6. 19 ◯ 18

7. 16 ◯ 10   8. 5 ◯ 11   9. 7 ◯ 9

Write each set of numbers in order from least to greatest.

10. 8   5   10   11. 18   12   6   12. 19   14   15

___ ___ ___   ___ ___ ___   ___ ___ ___

Write each set of numbers in order from greatest to least.

13. 4   12   9   14. 11   3   13   15. 9   19   16

___ ___ ___   ___ ___ ___   ___ ___ ___

16. **Logical Thinking** Use the clues and numbers
    in the box to solve the problem.

    Kyle has more hats than Sue.
    Kim has the most hats.
    How many hats does each child have?

    9 8
     5

    Kyle _____   Kim _____   Sue _____

Name _____

Targeted Practice

Find all of the equations for the Math Mountains.
Draw squiggles under the partners.

15

7   8

1. $7 + 8 = 15$  $15 = 7 + 8$

_____   _____

_____   _____

_____   _____

11

4   7

2. $4 + 7 = 11$  $11 = 4 + 7$

_____   _____

_____   _____

_____   _____

Compare and Order Numbers

Homework

$5 + 2 + 3 = \boxed{}$

You can add in three different ways.

$7 + 3$
$5 + 2 + 3 = \boxed{10}$

$5 + 5$
$5 + 2 + 3 = \boxed{10}$

$8 + 2$
$5 + 2 + 3 = \boxed{10}$

Add the three numbers.

1. $4 + 7 + 3 = \boxed{}$ $5 + 1 + 3 = \boxed{}$ $6 + 3 + 4 = \boxed{}$

2. $6 + 2 + 8 = \boxed{}$ $4 + 2 + 6 = \boxed{}$ $7 + 7 + 3 = \boxed{}$

3. $3 + 4 + 7 = \boxed{}$ $5 + 9 + 2 = \boxed{}$ $4 + 3 + 9 = \boxed{}$

4. $7 + 3 + 5 = \boxed{}$ $2 + 4 + 4 = \boxed{}$ $7 + 1 + 7 = \boxed{}$

5. $3 + 6 + 3 = \boxed{}$ $2 + 2 + 9 = \boxed{}$ $6 + 1 + 3 = \boxed{}$

6. $5 + 5 + 5 = \boxed{}$ $2 + 7 + 2 = \boxed{}$ $9 + 2 + 5 = \boxed{}$

7. **Explain Your Thinking** Draw a 7, 9, 16 Math Mountain. Tell how it can help you add or subtract.

_____

_____

_____

Name _____

Remembering

Solve the story problem.   **Show your work.**

1. Nancy rode her bike 7 miles. Yolanda rode her bike 6 more miles than Nancy. How many miles did Yolanda ride her bike?

bike

☐ _____
   label

Add or subtract 0 or 1.

2. $2 + 0 =$ ☐ $5 - 1 =$ ☐ $5 + 0 =$ ☐ $4 - 1 =$ ☐

3. $7 + 1 =$ ☐ $6 - 0 =$ ☐ $3 + 0 =$ ☐ $1 - 1 =$ ☐

4. $8 + 1 =$ ☐ $8 - 0 =$ ☐ $9 + 1 =$ ☐ $3 - 1 =$ ☐

Find all of the equations for the 11, 7, 4 Math Mountain.
Draw squiggles under the partners.

5.

11
7   4

$7 + 4 = 11$  $11 = 7 + 4$

_____   _____

_____   _____

_____   _____

Add Three Numbers

Homework

1. Draw pictures to show 2 or more different ways to make 16¢.

2. Draw pictures to show 2 or more different ways to make 20¢.

3. Look at the pattern.

5, 8, 11, 14, 17

Mio says the rule for the pattern is +3.
Dave says the rule for the pattern is +4.
Who is right? Explain.

_____

_____

Remembering

Solve the story problem.   **Show your work.**

1. Tony has 8 model cars. Chen has 6 more model cars than Tony. How many model cars does Chen have?

model car

☐ _____
        label

Add or subtract.

2. $\begin{array}{r} 8 \\ + 5 \\ \hline \end{array}$ $\begin{array}{r} 6 \\ + 5 \\ \hline \end{array}$ $\begin{array}{r} 7 \\ + 7 \\ \hline \end{array}$ $\begin{array}{r} 7 \\ + 8 \\ \hline \end{array}$ $\begin{array}{r} 6 \\ + 7 \\ \hline \end{array}$ $\begin{array}{r} 8 \\ + 9 \\ \hline \end{array}$

3. $\begin{array}{r} 16 \\ - 8 \\ \hline \end{array}$ $\begin{array}{r} 15 \\ - 9 \\ \hline \end{array}$ $\begin{array}{r} 18 \\ - 9 \\ \hline \end{array}$ $\begin{array}{r} 12 \\ - 8 \\ \hline \end{array}$ $\begin{array}{r} 11 \\ - 7 \\ \hline \end{array}$ $\begin{array}{r} 13 \\ - 5 \\ \hline \end{array}$

4. Find all of the equations for the 12, 9, 3 Math Mountain. Draw squiggles under the partners.

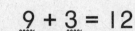

$9 + 3 = 12$

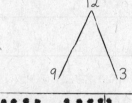

$12 = 9 + 3$

_____   _____

_____   _____

_____   _____

Use Mathematical Processes

Homework

1. Measure the horizontal line segment below
by marking and counting 1-cm lengths.

_____ ☐ cm

2. Draw a line segment 8 cm long.
Mark and count 1-cm lengths to check
the length.

Use your centimeter ruler to measure each vertical line segment.

3. | **4.** | **5.** |

☐ cm   ☐ cm   ☐ cm

---

6. On the Back Draw a 7-cm line segment.
Draw all the partner lengths. Write the partners
and the equation for each.

Rulers, Lengths, and Partner Lengths

Homework

Look for rectangles, squares, and triangles in your home and neighborhood.

1. List or draw objects that show squares.

2. List or draw objects that show rectangles.

3. List or draw objects that show triangles.

4. On the Back Draw a square, a rectangle, and a triangle

Squares, Rectangles, and Triangles

Homework

Use a centimeter ruler. Find the perimeter.

I.

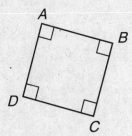

$P = \boxed{}$ cm

2.

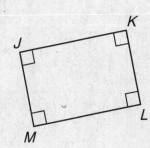

$P = \boxed{}$ cm

3.

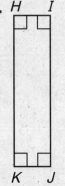

$P = \boxed{}$ cm

4.

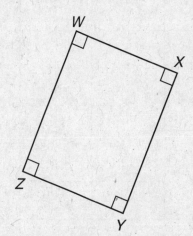

$P = \boxed{}$ cm

5. On the Back Draw a square and a rectangle.
Find the perimeter of each shape.

Perimeters of Squares and Rectangles

Use a centimeter ruler. Find the perimeter.

1.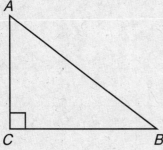

$P = \boxed{}$ cm

2.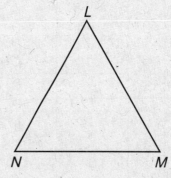

$P = \boxed{}$ cm

Measure. Round to the nearest centimeter.

3. _____ about $\boxed{}$ cm

4. _____ about $\boxed{}$ cm

Measure each side. Round to the nearest centimeter.
Find the perimeter.

5.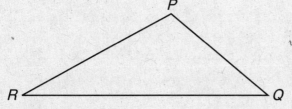

Perimeter is about $\boxed{}$ cm

6.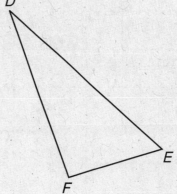

Perimeter is about $\boxed{}$ cm

7. On the Back Use a centimeter ruler. Draw three triangles.
Find the perimeter of each triangle.

Homework

Solve the story problems.   **Show your work.**

---

1. Brad had 14 toy boats. 5 of them floated away. How many does he have now?

   ☐ _____
       label

boat

---

2. Moses collected 17 rocks. He gave some of them away. Now he has 9 rocks left. How many did he give away?

   ☐ _____
       label

rock

---

3. Claire had 9 colored markers in her backpack when she left school. Some fell out on the way home. When she got home, she had only 5 markers. How many markers fell out of her backpack?

   ☐ _____
       label

backpack

---

4. A honeybee visited 7 flowers in the garden. Then it visited 5 more. How many flowers did the honeybee visit in all?

   ☐ _____
       label

honeybee

Remembering

1. Find all of the equations for the 15, 7, 8 Math Mountain.
Draw squiggles under each partner.

$7 + 8 = 15$ $15 = 7 + 8$

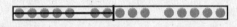

_____   _____

_____   _____

_____   _____

Add 3 numbers.

2. $4 + 1 + 4 = \boxed{}$ $5 + 1 + 1 = \boxed{}$ $2 + 2 + 4 = \boxed{}$

3. $5 + 2 + 2 = \boxed{}$ $4 + 1 + 3 = \boxed{}$ $2 + 3 + 2 = \boxed{}$

Add or subtract.

4.
$$\begin{array}{ccccc} 6 & 8 & 5 & 11 & 17 & 14 \\ +7 & +8 & +9 & -3 & -8 & -6 \\ \hline \end{array}$$

5. Measurement Use your centimeter ruler. On a
separate piece of paper, draw a square. Find its
perimeter.

Change Plus and Change Minus Story Problems

Homework

Make a math drawing to solve the story problems.

Show your work.

1. In the morning, Nick made 8 animals out of clay. In the afternoon, he made some more clay animals. Altogether, he made 15 clay animals. How many did he make in the afternoon?

clay animal

☐ _____
   label

2. Carrie saw some birds in a tree. 8 flew away. 5 were left. How many birds were in the tree first?

bird

☐ _____
   label

3. Leon and his friends made 12 snowmen. The next day, Leon saw that some of them had melted. Only 9 snowmen were left. How many melted?

snowmen

☐ _____
   label

4. 3 lizards sat on a rock in the sun. Then 9 more came out and sat on the rock. How many lizards are on the rock now?

rock

☐ _____
   label

Name _____

Targeted Practice

$5 + 4 + 3 =$ ☐

$9 \quad + 3$	$5 + \quad 7$	$8 + 4$
$5 + 4 + 3 = \boxed{12}$	$5 + 4 + 3 = \boxed{12}$	$5 + 4 + 3 = \boxed{12}$

Add.

1. $4 + 8 + 3 =$ ☐ $\qquad 8 + 8 + 2 =$ ☐ $\qquad 7 + 7 + 3 =$ ☐

2. $8 + 2 + 6 =$ ☐ $\qquad 5 + 4 + 9 =$ ☐ $\qquad 9 + 2 + 5 =$ ☐

3. $7 + 5 + 2 =$ ☐ $\qquad 8 + 4 + 2 =$ ☐ $\qquad 6 + 9 + 4 =$ ☐

4. $9 + 3 + 4 =$ ☐ $\qquad 9 + 4 + 5 =$ ☐ $\qquad 8 + 4 + 4 =$ ☐

5. $5 + 8 + 2 =$ ☐ $\qquad 2 + 9 + 6 =$ ☐ $\qquad 6 + 3 + 7 =$ ☐

6. $2 + 7 + 2 =$ ☐ $\qquad 5 + 4 + 5 =$ ☐ $\qquad 8 + 2 + 7 =$ ☐

7. $3 + 6 + 3 =$ ☐ $\qquad 9 + 2 + 2 =$ ☐ $\qquad 5 + 7 + 3 =$ ☐

8. $2 + 6 + 4 =$ ☐ $\qquad 6 + 3 + 4 =$ ☐ $\qquad 4 + 5 + 3 =$ ☐

9. $2 + 7 + 3 =$ ☐ $\qquad 4 + 2 + 5 =$ ☐ $\qquad 5 + 3 + 3 =$ ☐

More Change Plus and Change Minus Story Problems

Name _____

Homework

Make a math drawing to solve the story
problems.

Show your work.

1. There are some pigs on Mr. Smith's farm.
   8 of them are eating corn. The other 7 are
   drinking water. How many pigs are on Mr.
   Smith's farm?

   □ _____
        label

pig

2. Wendy bought 3 blue balloons and some
   red balloons for a party. She bought 11
   balloons. How many red ones did she
   buy?

   □ _____
        label

balloon

3. There are 14 children in the park. 7 of
   them are swinging. The rest are jumping
   rope. How many are jumping rope?

   □ _____
        label

jump rope

4. **Write Your Own** Write a collection story problem.
   Then draw a picture to solve it.

   _____

   _____

   _____

Remembering

Complete the Partner Houses.

1.

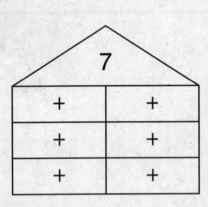

Add or subtract.

2.
$$\begin{array}{r} 4 \\ +7 \\ \hline \end{array}$$
$$\begin{array}{r} 5 \\ +6 \\ \hline \end{array}$$
$$\begin{array}{r} 7 \\ +8 \\ \hline \end{array}$$
$$\begin{array}{r} 8 \\ +6 \\ \hline \end{array}$$
$$\begin{array}{r} 7 \\ +7 \\ \hline \end{array}$$
$$\begin{array}{r} 9 \\ +5 \\ \hline \end{array}$$

3.
$$\begin{array}{r} 6 \\ +9 \\ \hline \end{array}$$
$$\begin{array}{r} 7 \\ +6 \\ \hline \end{array}$$
$$\begin{array}{r} 8 \\ +8 \\ \hline \end{array}$$
$$\begin{array}{r} 9 \\ +7 \\ \hline \end{array}$$
$$\begin{array}{r} 6 \\ +8 \\ \hline \end{array}$$
$$\begin{array}{r} 5 \\ +8 \\ \hline \end{array}$$

4.
$$\begin{array}{r} 13 \\ -8 \\ \hline \end{array}$$
$$\begin{array}{r} 12 \\ -7 \\ \hline \end{array}$$
$$\begin{array}{r} 17 \\ -9 \\ \hline \end{array}$$
$$\begin{array}{r} 14 \\ -6 \\ \hline \end{array}$$
$$\begin{array}{r} 15 \\ -7 \\ \hline \end{array}$$
$$\begin{array}{r} 16 \\ -8 \\ \hline \end{array}$$

5.
$$\begin{array}{r} 11 \\ -3 \\ \hline \end{array}$$
$$\begin{array}{r} 15 \\ -8 \\ \hline \end{array}$$
$$\begin{array}{r} 18 \\ -9 \\ \hline \end{array}$$
$$\begin{array}{r} 13 \\ -4 \\ \hline \end{array}$$
$$\begin{array}{r} 16 \\ -9 \\ \hline \end{array}$$
$$\begin{array}{r} 14 \\ -7 \\ \hline \end{array}$$

6. Measurement Use your centimeter ruler. On
a separate piece of paper, draw a segment
6 centimeters long. Draw all of its partner lengths.

Homework

Solve the story problems.   **Show your work.**

1. One bus has 6 girls and 7 boys on it. How
   many students are on the bus?

bus

   ☐ _____
         label

2. Pang bought some apples. Bill bought 6
   pears. Pang and Bill bought 13 pieces
   of fruit. How many apples did Pang buy?

pear

   ☐ _____
         label

3. Complete the Venn diagram by adding at least two
   things in the circle.

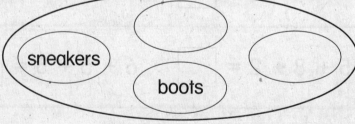

   _____
         Group Name

4. **Create Your Own** Use your Venn diagram to write
   your own group name story problem. Solve your
   problem with equations, words, or math drawings.

   _____

   _____

   _____

Name _____

Targeted Practice

$$2 + 3 + 6 = \boxed{11}$$

5 + 6	2 + 9	8 + 3
$2 + 3 + 6 = \boxed{11}$	$2 + 3 + 6 = \boxed{11}$	$2 + 3 + 6 = \boxed{11}$

Add.

1. $5 + 7 + 3 = \boxed{}$ $7 + 3 + 2 = \boxed{}$ $9 + 2 + 6 = \boxed{}$

2. $8 + 2 + 5 = \boxed{}$ $6 + 2 + 5 = \boxed{}$ $3 + 5 + 6 = \boxed{}$

3. $4 + 3 + 4 = \boxed{}$ $5 + 3 + 4 = \boxed{}$ $8 + 3 + 2 = \boxed{}$

4. $6 + 3 + 9 = \boxed{}$ $7 + 7 + 2 = \boxed{}$ $2 + 5 + 8 = \boxed{}$

5. $2 + 7 + 3 = \boxed{}$ $5 + 8 + 2 = \boxed{}$ $6 + 5 + 5 = \boxed{}$

6. $8 + 2 + 2 = \boxed{}$ $7 + 4 + 6 = \boxed{}$ $4 + 3 + 7 = \boxed{}$

7. $5 + 6 + 4 = \boxed{}$ $3 + 4 + 4 = \boxed{}$ $5 + 2 + 9 = \boxed{}$

8. $2 + 8 + 4 = \boxed{}$ $6 + 4 + 4 = \boxed{}$ $7 + 2 + 4 = \boxed{}$

9. $6 + 2 + 3 = \boxed{}$ $4 + 5 + 5 = \boxed{}$ $9 + 3 + 4 = \boxed{}$

Story Problems with Group Names

Homework

Make a math drawing to solve the story problems.   **Show your work.**

---

1. Peter has 13 eggs. Joe has 4 fewer than
Peter. How many eggs does Joe have?

☐ _____
         label

eggs

---

2. I want to give each of my 14 friends a
watermelon. I have 8 watermelons in my
garden. How many more do I need to
grow to give each friend a watermelon?

☐ _____
         label

watermelon

---

3. Lë has 5 lemons. Tina has 7 more than Lë.
How many lemons does Tina have?

☐ _____
         label

lemon

Write Your Own Complete this comparison story
problem. Then draw a picture to show how to
solve it.

4. I have 12 _____.

My friend has _____ fewer

_____ than I have. How many

_____ does my friend have?

☐ _____
         label

Remembering

Find all of the equations for the 13, 4, and 9
Math Mountain. Draw squiggles under the partners.

1.

$4 + 9 = 13$ 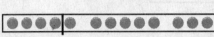 $13 = 4 + 9$

_____      _____

_____      _____

_____   _____

Solve the story problems.   **Show your work.**

2. 8 peppers are growing in Dana's garden.
   Dana has 9 peppers in the kitchen. How
   many peppers does Dana have altogether?

   [ ] _____
           label

pepper

3. Jonathan had 14 files on his CD. Then he
   deleted 6. How many files were left?

   [ ] _____
           label

CD

4. **Measurement** Use your centimeter ruler. On a separate
   piece of paper, draw a rectangle. Find its perimeter.

Name _____

Homework

Solve the story problems.

Show your work.

1. Parker and Natu went to the store to buy sunglasses. Parker paid $9 for his sunglasses. Natu paid $6 more than Parker. How much did Natu pay for his sunglasses?

sunglasses

[   ] _____
        label

2. A small ball costs 8 cents. A ring costs 8 more cents than the small ball. How many cents does a ring cost?

ring

[   ] _____
        label

3. If Jared gives away 3 strawberries, Jared will have as many strawberries as Phil. Phil has 8 strawberries. How many strawberries does Jared have?

strawberries

[   ] _____
        label

4. Andrew has 11 soccer balls. William has 3 soccer balls. How many fewer soccer balls does William have than Andrew?

soccer ball

[   ] _____
        label

Targeted Practice

Fill in the Venn diagrams to show some things
that belong together.

1.

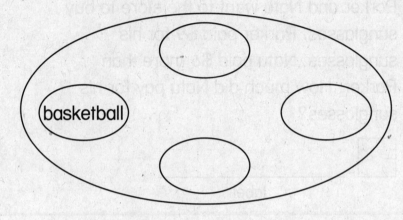

_____
        Group Name

2.

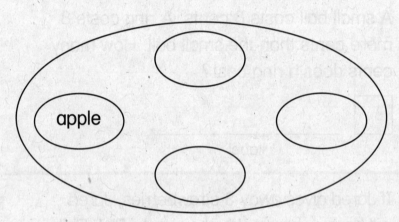

_____
        Group Name

3. You Decide Create your own Venn diagram.
   Write a group name.

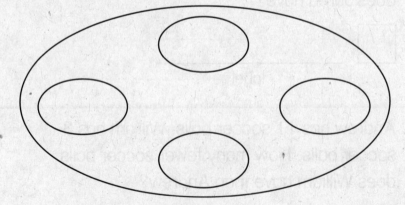

_____
        Group Name

Homework

Solve the story problems.   **Show your work.**

---

1. Susan rode her bicycle for 14 blocks. Awan rode his bicycle for 8 blocks. How many fewer blocks did Awan ride than Susan?

bicycle

☐ _____
    label

---

2. Eden has 7 blackberries. Her father gave her 9 more. How many blackberries does Eden have now?

blackberries

☐ _____
    label

---

3. There were 9 children on the bus. At the first bus stop, some children got off. 7 children are still on the bus. How many children got off at the first bus stop?

bus stop

☐ _____
    label

---

4. The clown had 12 balloons. He gave away 4 balloons. How many balloons did he keep?

balloons

☐ _____
    label

Name _____

Remembering

Add or subtract.

1. 4 + 1 = ☐   3 − 0 = ☐   6 + 0 = ☐   9 − 1 = ☐

2. 8 + 0 = ☐   7 − 1 = ☐   9 + 1 = ☐   4 − 0 = ☐

3. 7 + 1 = ☐   5 − 0 = ☐   4 + 0 = ☐   8 − 1 = ☐

Solve the story problem.   **Show your work.**

4. Mr. Tyson grilled 14 hot dogs. His family
   ate some. Now he has 6 hot dogs left.
   How many hot dogs did his family eat?

hot dog

☐ _____
     label

Complete the Partner Houses.

5.

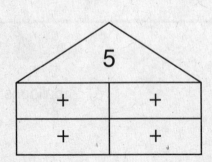 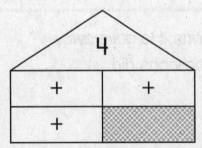

6. **Measurement** Use your centimeter ruler. On a separate
   piece of paper, draw a triangle. Find its perimeter.

Mixed Story Problems

Homework

For problems with not enough information, add
the information.

For problems with extra information, cross out the
extra information. Then solve the problem.

Show your work.

---

1. There are 14 children in music class.
Some children left to go to the library. How
many children are still in music class?

library

_____

☐ _____
       label

---

2. Rosa has 5 gold coins and 6 silver coins
in her collection. Her brother gave her 7
more gold coins. How many gold coins
does Rosa have in all?

coin

_____

☐ _____
       label

---

3. There were 7 bicycles in the rack at
school. Then some more children put their
bicycles in the rack. How many bicycles
are in the rack now?

bicycle

_____

☐ _____
       label

Targeted Practice

Solve the story problems.   **Show your work.**

1. Bernard had 9 acorns. Manuel had 6 fewer acorns than Bernard. How many acorns does Manuel have?

acorn

☐ _____
    label

2. Together Roma and Grace have 12 beads. Grace has 4 beads. How many beads does Grace have to buy to have the same as Roma?

beads

☐ _____
    label

3. There are 14 lions at the zoo. The zoo has to get 6 tigers to have as many tigers as lions. How many tigers does the zoo have?

lion

☐ _____
    label

4. There are 13 children on the baseball team. There are 7 children on the swim team. How many more children are on the baseball team than on the swim team?

baseball

☐ _____
    label

Name _____

Homework

Cross out the extra information or write hidden or missing information. Then solve the problems.

Show your work.

1. Joel knows the names of 9 different dinosaurs. His friend Peja knows the names of 6 dinosaurs and 8 birds. How many dinosaur names do the two friends know together?

dinosaur

☐ _____
    label

2. I have a ring for each finger of both hands. I want to buy 4 more rings. How many rings will I have then?

hands

☐ _____
    label

3. Erica had 6 coins in her coin collection. She went to a coin show this week and bought some more. How many coins does she have now?

coin

☐ _____
    label

Remembering

Find all of the equations for the 15, 6, 9 Math Mountain.
Draw squiggles under the partners.

1.

15

6   9

$\underline{6 + 9 = 15}$

$\underline{15 = 6 + 9}$

_____   _____

_____   _____

_____   _____

Solve the story problem.   **Show your work.**

2. Sofia has 13 pounds of grapes in her basket. She has 6 more pounds than Tony has in his basket. How many pounds of grapes are in Tony's basket?

grapes

☐ _____
    label

Make a ten or count on to find the partner.

3. 6 + ☐ = 13   17 − 9 = ☐   5 + ☐ = 14

4. 8 + ☐ = 15   14 − 6 = ☐   15 − 7 = ☐

5. **Measurement** Use your centimeter ruler. On a separate piece of paper, draw a rectangle. Find its perimeter.

Problems with Hidden Information and Mixed Practice

Name _____

Homework

Solve the story problems.

Show your work.

1. Bessie counted 5 fish, 3 turtles, and some
frogs. She counted 14 animals altogether.
How many frogs are there?

turtle

[ ] _____
　　　 label

2. Todd had 4 red blocks and 5 green blocks.
Then his sister gave him some blue blocks.
Todd has 17 blocks now. How many blue
blocks did his sister give him?

block

[ ] _____
　　　 label

3. There were 15 cups of water in the jug.
Jacob poured out 9 cups of water for
people at the race to drink. Then his uncle
put 7 more cups of water into the jug. How
many cups of water are in the jug now?

jug

[ ] _____
　　　 label

4. Megan had 12 dollars in her pocket. She
spent 6 dollars on lunch. Then a friend
gave her back the 3 dollars he borrowed
yesterday. How much money does Megan
have now?

lunch

[ ] _____
　　　 label

Targeted Practice

Solve the story problems.   **Show your work.**

---

1. Alvin had a dozen pretzels in his bag.
For lunch, he ate 9 of them. How many
pretzels does Alvin have left?

pretzel

☐ _____
        label

---

2. Ed has 10 pairs of shoes in his closet.
Alicia has a different pair of shoes for
each day of the week. How many pairs of
shoes do Ed and Alicia have together?

pair of
shoes

☐ _____
        label

---

3. Carlos has 8 parakeets as pets. Jeff
has a pair of parrots. How many birds
do Carlos and Jeff have together?

parakeet

☐ _____
        label

---

4. Samuel has 12 horseshoes in his shed.
He had to put all new horseshoes on his
horse today. How many horseshoes does
Samuel have left in his shed?

horseshoe

☐ _____
        label

Name _____

Homework

Solve the story problems.

Show your work.

1. Jerry ate 6 pieces of pizza. Then he ate 7 more pieces. Vesta ate 9 pieces of pizza. How many fewer pieces of pizza did Vesta eat than Jerry?

pizza

□ _____
label

2. Arnez has 2 angelfish and 5 goldfish. Carmen has 2 angelfish and 6 goldfish. How many more fish does Carmen have than Arnez?

angelfish

□ _____
label

3. Chin had 9 shrimp. He ate 3. Then his mother gave him 9 more. How many shrimp does Chin have now?

shrimp

□ _____
label

4. I bought 3 bananas, 5 apples, and some oranges. Altogether, I bought 15 pieces of fruit. How many oranges did I buy?

orange

□ _____
label

Name _____

Remembering

Add or subtract.

1.
$$\begin{array}{r} 7 \\ + 8 \\ \hline \end{array} \qquad \begin{array}{r} 6 \\ + 5 \\ \hline \end{array} \qquad \begin{array}{r} 9 \\ + 2 \\ \hline \end{array} \qquad \begin{array}{r} 7 \\ + 5 \\ \hline \end{array} \qquad \begin{array}{r} 6 \\ + 8 \\ \hline \end{array} \qquad \begin{array}{r} 3 \\ + 8 \\ \hline \end{array}$$

2.
$$\begin{array}{r} 13 \\ - 4 \\ \hline \end{array} \qquad \begin{array}{r} 15 \\ - 8 \\ \hline \end{array} \qquad \begin{array}{r} 17 \\ - 9 \\ \hline \end{array} \qquad \begin{array}{r} 16 \\ - 7 \\ \hline \end{array} \qquad \begin{array}{r} 18 \\ - 9 \\ \hline \end{array} \qquad \begin{array}{r} 11 \\ - 3 \\ \hline \end{array}$$

Solve the story problems.   **Show your work.**

3. Altogether, Adela and Ben have 13 pets.
   Ben has 6 dogs. Adela has some cats.
   How many cats does Adela have?

pets

   ☐ _____
          label

4. Lonnie planted 16 seeds in his backyard.
   4 were sunflower, 6 were tulip, and some
   were daisy. How many daisy seeds did
   he plant?

seeds

   ☐ _____
          label

5. **Measurement** Use your centimeter ruler. On a
   separate piece of paper, draw a segment 8 centimeters
   long. Draw all of its partner lengths.

Name _____

Solve the story problems.   **Show your work.**

school bus

1. The school bus will hold 16 children.
3 girls and 6 boys are already on the
bus. How many more children can fit on
the bus?

☐ _____
label

kite

2. Some kites flew in the air. Then 7 of them
got caught in trees. Now only 8 kites are
flying. How many kites were flying in the
beginning?

☐ _____
label

bubbles

3. Sheldon blew 13 bubbles. 6 of them
popped, so he blew 9 more bubbles.
How many bubbles are there now?

☐ _____
label

4. Explain Your Thinking Explain each step you
took to solve problem 3.

_____

_____

_____

Targeted Practice

Solve the story problems.   **Show your work.**

1. Rachel counted 4 cows, 3 goats, and some horses at the farm. She counted 16 animals. How many horses were at the farm?

cow

☐ _____
     label

2. Allison had 8 dollars in her pocket. Her mother gave her 7 more dollars. Then she spent 5 dollars on lunch. How much money does Allison have now?

dollar

☐ _____
     label

3. Students made 17 sandwiches for the picnic. They made 3 chicken sandwiches, 6 roast beef sandwiches, and some cheese sandwiches. How many cheese sandwiches did they make?

sandwich

☐ _____
     label

4. **Summarize** Explain each step you took to solve problem 3.

_____

_____

_____

                              Mixed Practice and Writing Story Problems

Name _____

Homework

Cross out any extra information.
Solve the story problems.

Show your work.

---

1. Edward and his sister read 15 books to
their little brother. Edward read 8 of them.
His sister ate 2 oranges while Edward
read. How many books did his sister read?

book

☐ _____
label

---

2. Amy had 5 good ideas while taking a walk.
Then she had some more good ideas while
riding her bike. Altogether she had a total
of 12 good ideas. How many good ideas
did she have while riding her bike?

bike

☐ _____
label

---

3. Valeria made 13 bracelets. 5 had beads in
them. The rest did not. How many bracelets
did not have any beads?

bracelet

☐ _____
label

---

4. Explain Choose one of the three problems.
Explain all of the steps you took to solve
the problem.

_____

_____

Name _____

Remembering

Solve the story problems.

Show your work.

1. Julio has 17 pairs of shorts. Brian has 9 pairs of shorts. How many more pairs of shorts does Brian need to get to have the same as Julio?

pair of shorts

☐ _____
   label

2. Shelby has 8 clocks in her house. Theo has 4 clocks in his house. There are 5 clocks in Heather's house. How many clocks do the three of them have altogether?

clock

☐ _____
   label

Add 3 numbers.

3. $3 + 8 + 2 = $ ☐ $2 + 3 + 6 = $ ☐ $2 + 9 + 4 = $ ☐

4. $7 + 7 + 4 = $ ☐ $6 + 6 + 4 = $ ☐ $4 + 7 + 3 = $ ☐

5. $6 + 2 + 4 = $ ☐ $9 + 7 + 2 = $ ☐ $6 + 5 + 3 = $ ☐

6. **Measurement** Use your centimeter ruler. On a separate piece of paper, draw a segment 10 centimeters long. Draw all of its partner lengths.

Mixed Practice

Homework

Tell if there is enough information to solve the problem.

If there is enough information, solve it.

If there is not enough information, tell what is needed.

1. I am thinking of a shape.

It has a perimeter of 16 cm.

What shape am I thinking of?

Is there enough information? Yes   No

_____

2. I am thinking of a number.

It is greater than 30. It is odd.

What number am I thinking of?

Is there enough information? Yes   No

_____

3. I am thinking of a shape.

Each side is 4 cm.

There are 4 sides.

What shape am I thinking of?

Is there enough information? Yes   No

_____

4. I am thinking of a number.

It has two partners.

One partner is 8. The other is 9.

What number am I thinking of?

Is there enough information? Yes   No

_____

Name _____

Remembering

Solve each story problem.

Show your work.

1. Carol has 17 horse statues. Bala has 8 horse statues. How many more horse statues does Bala need to get to have the same number as Carol?

horse statue

☐ _____

2. Roberto has 13 pieces of fruit. He has 6 oranges, 3 apples, and some bananas. How many bananas does he have?

fruit

☐ _____

Add 3 numbers.

3. $5 + 6 + 3 =$ ☐

4. ☐ $= 2 + 8 + 8$

5. $3 + 5 + 7 =$ ☐

6. $4 + 5 + 8 =$ ☐

7. ☐ $= 1 + 9 + 3$

8. $6 + 2 + 4 =$ ☐

9. $7 + 4 + 5 =$ ☐

10. ☐ $= 5 + 2 + 4$

11. $4 + 3 + 7 =$ ☐

12. Measurement Use your centimeter ruler. On a separate piece of paper, draw a segment 9 centimeters long. Draw all of its partner lengths.

Use Mathematical Processes

Homework

Use a centimeter ruler. Find the perimeter of each shape.

1.

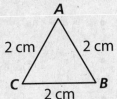

$P = \boxed{}$ cm

2.

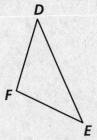

$P = \boxed{}$ cm

3.

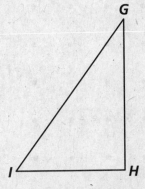

$P = \boxed{}$ cm

4.

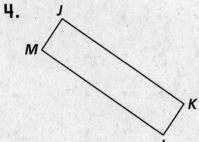

$P = \boxed{}$ cm

5.

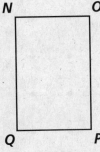

$P = \boxed{}$ cm

6.

$P = \boxed{}$ cm

7.

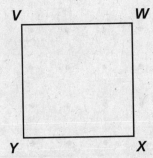

$P = \boxed{}$ cm

8.

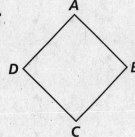

$P = \boxed{}$ cm

9.

$P = \boxed{}$ cm

10. **On the Back** Draw three triangles.
  - In the first triangle, all sides have the same length.
  - In the second triangle, only two sides have the same length.
  - In the third triangle, each side has a different length.

Share Observations About Geometry

Name _____

Homework

In each row draw three more parallelograms.
The first row is done for you.

1.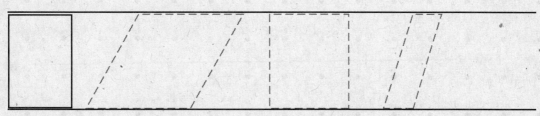

2.

3.

4.

5.

 6. On the Back Draw three different parallelograms.

Define Parallel Lines and Parallelograms **85**

Define Parallel Lines and Parallelograms

Homework

Name _____

Place a check mark beside each word that names the shape.

1.

☐ quadrilateral

☐ parallelogram

☐ rectangle

☐ square

2.

☐ quadrilateral

☐ parallelogram

☐ rectangle

☐ square

3.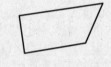

☐ quadrilateral

☐ parallelogram

☐ rectangle

☐ square

4.

☐ quadrilateral

☐ parallelogram

☐ rectangle

☐ square

5.

☐ quadrilateral

☐ parallelogram

☐ rectangle

☐ square

6.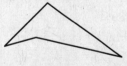

☐ quadrilateral

☐ parallelogram

☐ rectangle

☐ square

7. On the Back Draw three different quadrilaterals that have the same perimeter.

Homework

Name _____

1. Write the numbers going down to see the tens.

1	11			41			71		
2									92
3						63			
				44			74		
		25							95
					56				
			37						
	18							88	
						69			
10	20			50					100

2. What number comes after 100? _____

3. What number comes next? _____

Targeted Practice

Solve each story problem.   **Show your work.**

1. Rama bought 6 onions and 8 carrots.
Teresa bought 5 eggplants. How many
fewer vegetables did Teresa buy than
Rama?

eggplant

☐ _____
      label

2. There were 18 people at Melvin's party.
7 were girls and the rest were boys. Then
5 boys left. How many boys are still at
the party?

party hat

☐ _____
      label

3. There are 9 computers in the computer
lab. 7 girls and 8 boys want to use the
computers. How many children do not get
to use a computer?

computer

☐ _____
      label

4. Melissa has 4 red feathers, 5 purple
feathers, and some yellow feathers in her
hat. She has 16 feathers in total. How
many feathers are yellow?

feather

☐ _____
      label

Homework

Add.

1. $50 + 40 =$ _____ $80 + 10 =$ _____ $60 + 20 =$ _____

   $5 + 4 =$ _____ $8 + 1 =$ _____ $6 + 2 =$ _____

2. $10 + 70 =$ _____ $30 + 70 =$ _____ $40 + 30 =$ _____

   $1 + 7 =$ _____ $3 + 7 =$ _____ $4 + 3 =$ _____

3. $30 + 60 =$ _____ $20 + 80 =$ _____ $50 + 40 =$ _____

   $3 + 6 =$ _____ $2 + 8 =$ _____ $5 + 4 =$ _____

4. $50 + 30 =$ _____ $70 + 20 =$ _____ $40 + 60 =$ _____

   $5 + 3 =$ _____ $7 + 2 =$ _____ $4 + 6 =$ _____

5. $90 + 10 =$ _____ $50 + 20 =$ _____ $20 + 30 =$ _____

   $9 + 1 =$ _____ $5 + 2 =$ _____ $2 + 3 =$ _____

6. $30 + 10 =$ _____ $50 + 30 =$ _____ $40 + 20 =$ _____

   $3 + 1 =$ _____ $5 + 3 =$ _____ $4 + 2 =$ _____

Name _____

Remembering

Fill in the Venn diagram to show some things that belong together.

1.

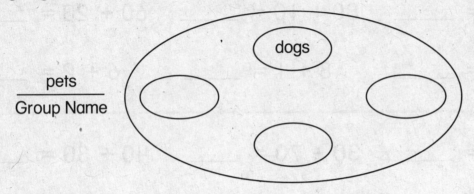

pets
‾‾‾‾‾‾‾‾
Group Name

Write the Math Mountain equations. Draw squiggles under the partners.

2.

12
8 4

$8 + 4 = 12$  $12 = 8 + 4$

_____      _____

_____      _____

_____      _____

Add or subtract.

3. $5 + 0 =$ ____ $10 - 0 =$ ____ $2 - 1 =$ ____

4. $2 + 1 =$ ____ $4 - 0 =$ ____ $9 + 1 =$ ____

5. **Measurement** On a separate piece of paper, draw 3 shapes with the same perimeter.

Draw Quick Tens and Quick Hundreds

Homework

Draw these numbers using hundred boxes, ten sticks,
and circles. Then write the hundreds, tens, and ones.

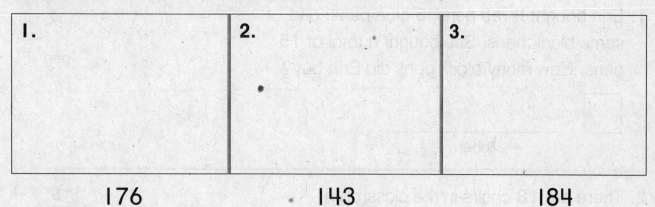

1.	2.	3.

176   143   184

$\underline{100} + \underline{70} + \underline{6}$ ___ + ___ + ___   ___ + ___ + ___

What numbers are shown here?   H = Hundreds, T = Tens, O = Ones

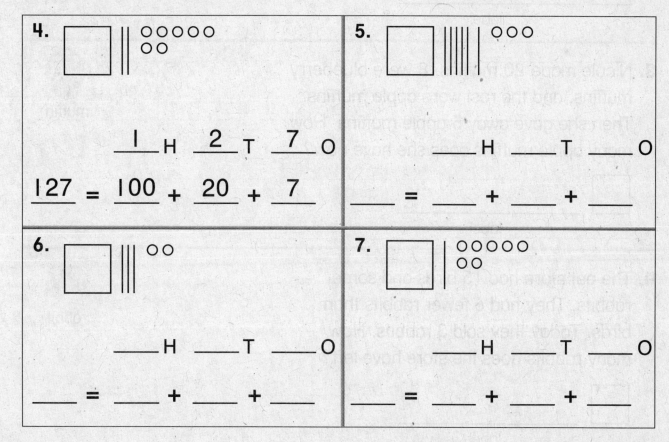

4.

$\underline{1}$ H $\underline{2}$ T $\underline{7}$ O

$\underline{127} = \underline{100} + \underline{20} + \underline{7}$

5.

___ H   ___ T   ___ O

___ = ___ + ___ + ___

6.

___ H   ___ T   ___ O

___ = ___ + ___ + ___

7.

___ H   ___ T   ___ O

___ = ___ + ___ + ___

Targeted Practice

Solve each story problem.

Show your work.

1. Erin bought 4 red pens, 5 blue pens, and some black pens. She bought a total of 15 pens. How many black pens did Erin buy?

pen

☐ _____
label

2. There are 18 chairs in the classroom. 7 boys and 6 girls need to sit in the classroom. How many chairs will not be used?

chair

☐ _____
label

3. Nicole made 20 muffins. 8 were blueberry muffins, and the rest were apple muffins. Then she gave away 5 apple muffins. How many apple muffins does she have now?

muffin

☐ _____
label

4. The pet store had 15 birds and some rabbits. They had 6 fewer rabbits than birds. Today they sold 3 rabbits. How many rabbits does the store have left?

rabbit

☐ _____
label

Represent Numbers in Different Ways

Add.

1. 25 + 7 = ____   2. 24 + 3 = ____   3. 73 + 3 = ____

4. 37 + 6 = ____   5. 59 + 5 = ____   6. 69 + 4 = ____

7. 26 + 8 = ____   8. 67 + 8 = ____   9. 37 + 2 = ____

10. 33 + 7 = ____   11. 56 + 6 = ____   12. 47 + 5 = ____

---

13. 40 + 60 = ____   20 + 80 = ____   30 + 30 = ____

    4 + 6 = ____   2 + 8 = ____   3 + 3 = ____

---

14. 50 + 20 = ____   70 + 20 = ____   40 + 80 = ____

    5 + 2 = ____   7 + 2 = ____   4 + 8 = ____

---

15. 50 + 40 = ____   60 + 20 = ____   20 + 30 = ____

    5 + 4 = ____   6 + 2 = ____   2 + 3 = ____

---

16. 30 + 60 = ____   10 + 50 = ____   40 + 40 = ____

    3 + 6 = ____   1 + 5 = ____   4 + 4 = ____

Remembering

Add the 3 numbers.

1. $3 + 2 + 6 =$ _____

2. $6 + 3 + 3 =$ _____

3. $7 + 3 + 2 =$ _____

4. $3 + 5 + 6 =$ _____

5. $9 + 4 + 2 =$ _____

6. $5 + 6 + 3 =$ _____

7. $5 + 8 + 5 =$ _____

8. $8 + 3 + 7 =$ _____

9. $3 + 9 + 6 =$ _____

10. $7 + 3 + 7 =$ _____

11. $9 + 3 + 3 =$ _____

12. $8 + 5 + 4 =$ _____

Complete the Partner Houses.

13.
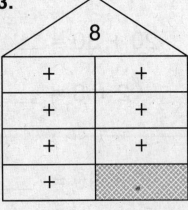

14.
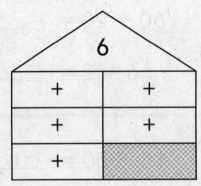

15.

16. **Measurement** On a separate piece of paper, draw
   3 shapes with the same perimeter.

Add 2-Digit and 1-Digit Numbers

Name _____

Homework

Group the 10-partners. The first one is done for you.

1. 3 + 7 = 10

2. 9 + 1 = 10

○○○○○ ○○○○○

3. 4 + 6 = 10

○○○○○ ○○○○○

Group the 100-partners. The first one is done for you.

4. 30 + 70 = 100

5. 90 + 10 = 100

6. 40 + 60 = 100

Add.

7. 80 + 60 = _____   60 + 90 = _____   60 + 70 = _____

8 + 6 = _____   6 + 9 = _____   6 + 7 = _____

8. 70 + 50 = _____   30 + 90 = _____   90 + 60 = _____

7 + 5 = _____   3 + 9 = _____   9 + 6 = _____

9. 40 + 90 = _____   90 + 80 = _____   80 + 50 = _____

4 + 9 = _____   9 + 8 = _____   8 + 5 = _____

Name _____

Targeted Practice

Cross out the extra information.
Solve each story problem.

Show your work.

---

1. There were 6 trains and 2 buses at Main Street Station. 9 more buses and 4 more trains just arrived. How many buses are at the station now?

bus station

☐ _____
          label

---

2. The pet store had 12 kittens and 11 puppies. Today they sold 3 puppies. How many puppies does the pet store still have?

kitten

☐ _____
          label

---

3. The farmer has 8 cows and 6 turkeys. He just bought 7 more turkeys. How many turkeys does the farmer have now?

turkey

☐ _____
          label

---

4. Jane checked out 9 nature books and 7 adventure books from the library. Then she returned 5 nature books. How many nature books does she still have?

nature book

☐ _____
          label

Find Decade Partners

Name _____

Homework

Solve each story problem.

---

1. Mina picked 63 flowers from her garden. She can put 10 flowers in each vase. How many vases will be filled up? How many extra flowers will she have?

☐ vases   ☐ extra flowers

---

2. Luisa has 85 coupons. She can trade in 10 of them for a toy. How many toys can Luisa get for her coupons? How many coupons will she have left over?

☐ toys   ☐ coupons left over

---

3. Mustafa wants to buy books that cost 10 dollars each. He has 45 dollars. How many books can he buy? How many dollars will he have left over?

☐ books   ☐ dollars left over

---

4. The track team has 72 water bottles. They pack them 10 to a box. How many boxes can they fill with bottles? How many water bottles will be left over?

☐ boxes   ☐ water bottles left over

Name _____

Remembering

What numbers are shown here?

H = Hundreds, T = Tens, O = Ones

1. ☐ ‖‖‖ °°	**2.** ☐ ‖‖‖ °°°°° °°°°
___ H ___ T ___ O	___ H ___ T ___ O
___ = ___ + ___ + ___	___ = ___ + ___ + ___
3. ☐ ‖‖‖‖‖ °°°	**4.** ☐ ‖ °°°°°
___ H ___ T ___ O	___ H ___ T ___ O
___ = ___ + ___ + ___	___ = ___ + ___ + ___

Solve each story problem.   **Show your work.**

5. Lee bought 7 pencils on Friday. On Saturday she bought 3 erasers and 4 pencils. How many pencils did she buy altogether on those two days?

☐ _____
     label

pencil

6. Corey saw 5 ducks. James saw 13 ducks. How many fewer ducks did Corey see than James?

☐ _____
     label

duck

7. Measurement On a separate piece of paper, draw 3 shapes with the same perimeter.

Combine Ones, Tens, and Hundreds

Homework

Draw lines to make pairs.
Write odd or even.

1.

_____

2.

_____

3. ●●●●
●●●●

_____

4. ●●●●●●●
●●●●●●●●

_____

Write odd or even for each number.

5. 18 _____

6. 60 _____

7. 49 _____

8. 32 _____

9. 51 _____

10. 87 _____

Name _____

Remembering

What numbers are shown here?

1. ☐ | | | | ○ ○ ○

   ____ H ____ T ____ O

   ____ = ____ + ____ + ____

2. ☐ | | | | | | | ○ ○ ○ ○ ○ ○

   ____ H ____ T ____ O

   ____ = ____ + ____ + ____

3. ☐ | | ○ ○ ○ ○

   ____ H ____ T ____ O

   ____ = ____ + ____ + ____

4. ☐ | | | | | ○ ○ ○ ○ ○ ○ ○ ○

   ____ H ____ T ____ O

   ____ = ____ + ____ + ____

Solve each story problem.

Show your work.

5. Ramon has 15 baseball cards. Michael has 9 cards. How many fewer cards does Michael have than Ramon?

   ☐ _____
   label

card

6. Ming has 5 stickers on 1 sheet. 2 stickers are stars. She has 4 stickers on the second sheet. How many stickers does she have on the two sheets?

   ☐ _____
   label

☺
sticker

Odd and Even Numbers

Homework

Circle a group of 10. Estimate how many in all. Count.

1.

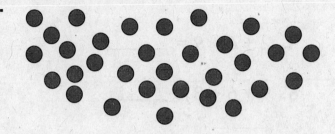

Estimate _____

Actual _____

2.

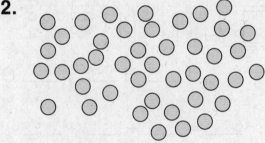

Estimate _____

Actual _____

Estimate how many pennies will fit in the rectangle.
Place pennies to fill the rectangle. Count the pennies.

3.

Estimate _____

Actual _____

Remembering

Add the 3 numbers.

1. $4 + 2 + 7 =$ _____

2. $3 + 2 + 9 =$ _____

3. $5 + 7 + 3 =$ _____

4. $2 + 6 + 9 =$ _____

5. $3 + 2 + 6 =$ _____

6. $9 + 6 + 3 =$ _____

7. $5 + 4 + 7 =$ _____

8. $8 + 1 + 9 =$ _____

What numbers are shown here?

9.  □ | | | | | | ° ° ° °

___ H ___ T ___ O

___ = ___ + ___ + ___

10.  □ | | | | | | | | | ° ° ° °°°

___ H ___ T ___ O

___ = ___ + ___ + ___

11.  □ | | | ° °

___ H ___ T ___ O

___ = ___ + ___ + ___

12.  □ | | | | | | | | | ° ° ° ° °°

___ H ___ T ___ O

___ = ___ + ___ + ___

Estimation

Homework

Name _____

Add ones, tens, or a hundred.

1.   9 + 8 = _____   7 + 7 = _____   9 + 5 = _____

    90 + 80 = _____   70 + 70 = _____   90 + 50 = _____

2.   6 + 8 = _____   8 + 3 = _____   9 + 7 = _____

    60 + 80 = _____   80 + 30 = _____   90 + 70 = _____

3.   7 + 5 = _____   6 + 9 = _____   8 + 8 = _____

    70 + 50 = _____   60 + 90 = _____   80 + 80 = _____

4.   8 + 7 = _____   6 + 5 = _____   9 + 4 = _____

    80 + 70 = _____   60 + 50 = _____   90 + 40 = _____

5. 100 + 48 = _____   6. 21 + 100 = _____   7. 100 + 2 = _____

    10 + 48 = _____   21 + 10 = _____   10 + 2 = _____

    1 + 48 = _____   21 + 1 = _____   1 + 2 = _____

Targeted Practice

Add.

1. 28
 + 19

   52
 + 33

   59
 + 27

2. 45
 + 16

   54
 + 37

   38
 + 21

3. 25
 + 62

   23
 + 48

   55
 + 35

4. 77
 + 14

   56
 + 29

   41
 + 38

Invent 2-Digit Addition

Homework

Name _____

Solve the story problems.   **Show your work.**

---

1. Kivy made 34 baskets. Her father made 58 baskets. How many baskets did they make in all?

basket

☐ _____
      label

---

2. Glen printed 67 posters yesterday and 86 more today. How many posters did he print in total?

poster

☐ _____
      label

Add.

3.   39   67   47
       + 44   + 56   + 98

---

4.   48   85   94
       + 33   + 68   + 57

Remembering

Add.

1. $7 + 3 =$ _____ $6 + 9 =$ _____ $8 + 3 =$ _____

    $70 + 30 =$ _____ $60 + 90 =$ _____ $80 + 30 =$ _____

---

2. $6 + 6 =$ _____ $4 + 8 =$ _____ $9 + 9 =$ _____

    $60 + 60 =$ _____ $40 + 80 =$ _____ $90 + 90 =$ _____

---

3. $6 + 4 =$ _____ $5 + 2 =$ _____ $100 + 14 =$ _____

    $60 + 40 =$ _____ $50 + 20 =$ _____ $10 + 14 =$ _____

                                            $1 + 14 =$ _____

Draw these numbers using boxes, sticks, and circles.
Then write the hundreds, tens, and ones.

4.

127

$\underline{100} + \underline{20} + \underline{7}$

5.

109

___ + ___ + ___

6.

133

___ + ___ + ___

7. Measurement On a separate piece of paper, draw
3 shapes with the same perimeter.

Addition–Show All Totals Method

Homework

```
  86    or    86
+ 57       + 57
 130        143
+ 13
 143
```

130 + 13 = 143

Add. Use any method.

1.
```
  97
+ 45
```

```
  54
+ 39
```

```
  35
+ 47
```

2.
```
  56
+ 77
```

```
  76
+ 88
```

```
  86
+ 65
```

3.
```
  47
+ 73
```

```
  87
+ 49
```

```
  57
+ 48
```

Addition—New Groups Below Method **109**

Targeted Practice

Solve each story problem.   **Show your work.**

---

1. Greg had some library books. He took
   8 books back to the library. Now he has
   8 books. How many books did he have
   in the beginning?

library

   ☐ _____
              label

---

2. Asha drew some pictures. Then she drew
   5 more pictures. Now she has 14 pictures.
   How many did she draw first?

picture

   ☐ _____
              label

---

3. Sam's mom gave him some crackers. He
   ate 9 crackers. He has 6 crackers left.
   How many crackers did his mom give
   him?

crackers

   ☐ _____
              label

---

4. Some children were playing at the park.
   7 children came. There are 14 children
   playing at the park now. How many
   children were playing at the park to start?

park

   ☐ _____
              label

Addition–New Groups Below Method

Homework

```
   75        75
+  49     +  49
-------    -------
  110       124
+  14
-------
  124  or
```

110 + 14 = 124

Add. Use any method.

1.
```
   83           65           78
+  79        +  47        +  34
```

2.
```
   74           48           92
+  99        +  87        +  59
```

3.
```
   63           75           86
+  77        +  48        +  32
```

Practice Addition with Totals Over 100 **111**

Remembering

Solve each story problem.   **Show your work.**

---

1. The Denny Tree Farm has 84 pine trees.
Baker's Acres has 37 pine trees. How
many pine trees do both places have?

pine tree

☐ _____
        label

---

2. Lin found some shells. Lee found 9 more
shells. They now have 17 shells. How
many shells did Lin find?

shell

☐ _____
        label

---

3. The jewelry store has 48 watches on sale.
The pharmacy next door has 23 watches on
sale. How many watches do the two stores
have to sell in all?

watch

☐ _____
        label

---

4. The Day Care Center has 29 teddy bears.
They just ordered 75 more. How many
teddy bears will the Day Care Center have
when the order comes in?

teddy bear

☐ _____
        label

---

5. Measurement On a separate piece of paper, draw
3 shapes with the same perimeter.

Homework

Be the helper. Is the answer OK? Write *yes* or *no*.
If *no,* fix the mistakes and write the correct answer.

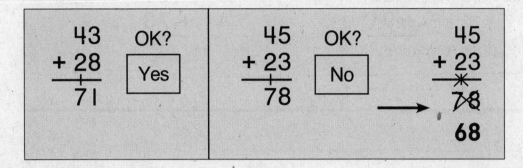

```
    43      OK?         45     OK?              45
  + 28    ┌─────┐     + 23   ┌─────┐          + 23
  ──┼──   │ Yes │     ──┼──  │ No  │          ──*──
    71    └─────┘       78   └─────┘    ──→     7̶8̶
                                                68
```

1. 27   OK?
  + 45   ┌─────┐
  ──┼──   │   │
    72   └─────┘

2. 68   OK?
  + 26   ┌─────┐
  ──┼──   │   │
    84   └─────┘

3. 32   OK?
  + 29   ┌─────┐
  ─────   │   │
    511   └─────┘

4. 16   OK?
  + 67   ┌─────┐
  ──2──   │   │
    91   └─────┘

5. 59   OK?
  + 25   ┌─────┐
  ─────   │   │
    74   └─────┘

6. 51   OK?
  + 44   ┌─────┐
  ─────   │   │
    95   └─────┘

7. 85   OK?
  + 56   ┌─────┐
  ──┼──   │   │
    141   └─────┘

8. 58   OK?
  + 99   ┌─────┐
  ─────   │   │
    147   └─────┘

9. 73   OK?
  + 82   ┌─────┐
  ──┼──   │   │
    165   └─────┘

Name _____

Targeted Practice

Add. Use any method.

1.
$$
\begin{array}{r} 42 \\ +\ 74 \\ \hline \end{array}
\qquad
\begin{array}{r} 88 \\ +\ 91 \\ \hline \end{array}
\qquad
\begin{array}{r} 61 \\ +\ 73 \\ \hline \end{array}
$$

2.
$$
\begin{array}{r} 75 \\ +\ 33 \\ \hline \end{array}
\qquad
\begin{array}{r} 42 \\ +\ 97 \\ \hline \end{array}
\qquad
\begin{array}{r} 27 \\ +\ 71 \\ \hline \end{array}
$$

3.
$$
\begin{array}{r} 95 \\ +\ 61 \\ \hline \end{array}
\qquad
\begin{array}{r} 22 \\ +\ 93 \\ \hline \end{array}
\qquad
\begin{array}{r} 81 \\ +\ 71 \\ \hline \end{array}
$$

4.
$$
\begin{array}{r} 36 \\ +\ 92 \\ \hline \end{array}
\qquad
\begin{array}{r} 82 \\ +\ 75 \\ \hline \end{array}
\qquad
\begin{array}{r} 54 \\ +\ 73 \\ \hline \end{array}
$$

Choose an Addition Method

Homework

Solve each story problem.

1. Here is the path Fluffy took on her walk today. How many yards did she walk?

   ☐ _____
        label

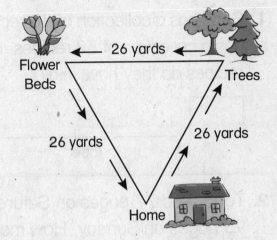

Flower Beds ← 26 yards ← Trees

26 yards   26 yards

Home

---

2. Colin wants to decorate a picture frame with gold ribbon. How long should the ribbon be if he wants to outline the whole frame?

   ☐ _____
        label

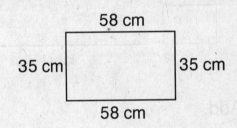

58 cm

35 cm   35 cm

58 cm

---

3. Here is a top view drawing of the new sandbox for the park. Each side is 16 feet long. A wooden seat runs along the perimeter. How long is the seat?

   ☐ _____
        label

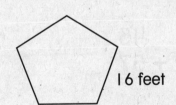

16 feet

Name _____

Remembering

Solve each story problem.

Show your work.

1. Sean has a collection of 48 recipes. Hannah has a collection of 53 recipes. How many recipes do they have in all?

recipes

[ ] _____
　　　　　label

2. Todd read 77 pages on Saturday. He read 93 pages on Sunday. How many pages did he read in the two days?

pages

[ ] _____
　　　　　label

Add.

3.   64   19   13
  + 87   + 78   + 79

4.   45   26   86
  + 57   + 97   + 59

5. **Measurement** On a separate piece of paper, draw 3 shapes with the same perimeter.

　　　　　　　　2-Digit Addition in Perimeter Problems

Homework

Here are some more fruits and vegetables from the
Farm Stand. Answer the questions below. Then draw
the money amount. The first one is done for you.

Apples 79¢	Eggplant 96¢	Pears 58¢	Green Onions 67¢	Oranges 85¢

How much would you spend if you wanted to buy

1. apples and
oranges? _____164_____ ¢ | I dollar | (10¢) (10¢) (10¢) (10¢) (10¢) (10¢)
(1¢) (1¢) (1¢) (1¢)

2. apples and
green onions? _____ ¢

3. pears and
green onions? _____ ¢

4. pears and
apples? _____ ¢

5. eggplant and
oranges? _____ ¢

Targeted Practice

Under the coins write the total amount of money so far.
The first one is done for you.

1. 10¢   10¢   5¢   5¢   1¢   1¢

10¢   20¢   25¢   30¢   31¢   32¢

2. 10¢   10¢   10¢   10¢   10¢   1¢

_____ _____ _____ _____ _____ _____

3. 10¢   5¢   5¢   5¢   1¢   1¢   1¢

_____ _____ _____ _____ _____ _____ _____

4. 10¢   5¢   1¢   1¢   1¢   1¢

_____ _____ _____ _____ _____ _____

5. Draw the coins you could use to show 85¢.
Use , , and Ⓟ.

Buy with Pennies and Dimes

Here are some more foods from the snack bar. Answer
the questions below. Then draw the money amounts
using dollars, dimes, nickels, and pennies.

| Hot Dog 87¢ | Peach 76¢ | Sandwich 98¢ | Corn on the Cob 65¢ | Watermelon 59¢ |

How much would you spend if you wanted to buy

1. a hot dog and
corn on the cob? _____ ¢

2. a sandwich and
a peach? _____ ¢

3. watermelon and
a hot dog? _____ ¢

4. a sandwich and
watermelon? _____ ¢

5. Problem Solving Ivan has 6 coins. The value of his
coins is 37¢. Three of his coins are dimes.
What are the other 3 coins?

_____

Name _____

Remembering

Solve each story problem.   **Show your work.**

---

1. There are 53 green peppers in the
vegetable bin. There are 59 yellow
peppers in the vegetable bin. How many
green and yellow peppers are there in all?

peppers

☐ _____
          label

---

2. Seth found some rocks in a field. Mandy
found 5 more rocks. There are now 13
rocks. How many rocks did Seth find?

rocks

☐ _____
          label

---

3. Ted's Trucking Company had 84 trucks.
They just bought 28 new trucks. How
many trucks do they have now?

truck

☐ _____
          label

Add.

4.   49   93   61
     + 85   + 56   + 39
     ____   ____   ____

5. Measurement On a separate piece of paper, draw 3
shapes with the same perimeter.

Buy with Pennies, Nickels, and Dimes

Homework

Complete the number sequence. Write the rule.

1. 12, 14, 16, _____ , _____ , _____ , _____   Rule: n _+ 2_

2. 25, 30, 35, _____ , _____ , _____ , _____   Rule: n _____

3. 49, 52, 55, _____ , _____ , _____ , _____   Rule: n _____

4. 80, 90, 100, _____ , _____ , _____ , _____   Rule: n _____

5. 46, 56, 66, _____ , _____ , _____ , _____   Rule: n _____

6. 58, 56, 54, _____ , _____ , _____ , _____   Rule: n _− 2_

7. 39, 36, 33, _____ , _____ , _____ , _____   Rule: n _____

8. 48, 42, 36, _____ , _____ , _____ , _____   Rule: n _____

9. 70, 65, 60, _____ , _____ , _____ , _____   Rule: n _____

10. 126, 130, 134, _____ , _____ , _____ , _____   Rule: n _____

11. 135, 140, 145, _____ , _____ , _____ , _____   Rule: n _____

12. Explain Your Thinking Which takes less time? Explain.
- Skip count by 2s from 2 to 100.
- Skip count by 5s from 5 to 100.

_____

_____

Name

Targeted Practice

Complete the number sequence. Write the rule.

1. 15, 21, 27, _____, _____, _____   Rule: n **+ 6**

2. 39, 35, 31, _____, _____, _____   Rule: n _____

3. 29, 34, 39, _____, _____, _____   Rule: n _____

4. 43, 39, 35, _____, _____, _____   Rule: n _____

5. 66, 69, 72, _____, _____, _____   Rule: n _____

6. 43, 35, 27, _____, _____, _____   Rule: n _____

7. 84, 86, 88, _____, _____, _____   Rule: n _____

8. 52, 46, 40, _____, _____, _____   Rule: n _____

9. 21, 29, 37, _____, _____, _____   Rule: n _____

10. 90, 87, 84, _____, _____, _____   Rule: n _____

11. 11, 17, 23, _____, _____, _____   Rule: n _____

12. 49, 56, 63, _____, _____, _____   Rule: n _____

13. 37, 48, 59, _____, _____, _____   Rule: n _____

14. 84, 75, 66, _____, _____, _____   Rule: n _____

Sequences

Name _____

Homework

Solve each story problem.   **Show your work.**

1. The theater can hold 100 people. We sold
62 tickets to the play. How many more
tickets do we have to sell to fill the theater?

theater

☐ _____
          label

2. My orchard has 82 trees in it. 47 are lime
trees. The rest are lemon trees. How many
lemon trees do I have?

orchard

☐ _____
          label

3. There are 75 seats on the airplane. 41 of
them are near a window. The rest are not.
How many seats are not near a window?

window

☐ _____
          label

4. The gift store sold 93 plant and animal key
chains. 48 were plant key chains. How
many were animal key chains?

key chain

☐ _____
          label

5. Find the unknown partner.

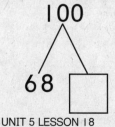
100
68 ☐

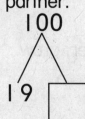
100
19 ☐

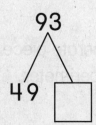
93
49 ☐

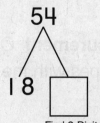
54
18 ☐

Remembering

Here are some more foods from the snack bar. Answer
the questions below. Then draw the money amount.

Hot Dog 87¢	Grapes 78¢	Yogurt 68¢	Popcorn 45¢	Fruit Juice 79¢

How much would you spend if you wanted to buy

1. fruit juice and
   a hot dog?　　_____ ¢

2. yogurt and
   popcorn?　　_____ ¢

Solve the story problem.　　　　　**Show your work.**

3. Dora caught 4 butterflies in her net. Joel
   caught some more butterflies. Now there
   are 13 butterflies. How many butterflies
   did Joel catch?

butterflies

   [ ]　_____
   　　　label

4. **Measurement** On a separate piece of paper, draw
   3 shapes with the same perimeter.

　　　　　　　　Find 2-Digit Partners

Name _____

Homework

Draw the next shape. Then write the name of the shape.

1.  ____

_____

2. 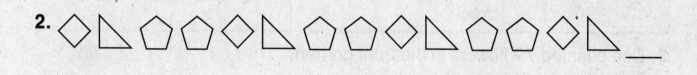 ____

_____

3. Draw an ABBC shape pattern.

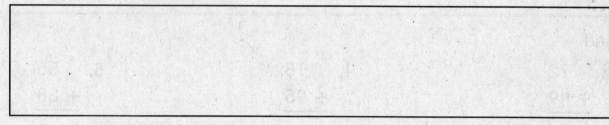

Say each pattern aloud.
Write the next number.

4. 1, 2, 3, 1, 2, 3, 1, 2, 3, 1, 2, _____

5. 7, 7, 8, 7, 7, 8, 7, 7, 8, 7, _____

6. 4, 4, 5, 6, 4, 4, 5, 6, 4, 4, 5, 6, 4, _____

7. 3, 4, 5, 6, 3, 4, 5, 6, 3, 4, 5, 6, 3, _____

Remembering

Solve each story problem.

Show your work.

1. Peter has 64 pennies in one bank. He has 58 pennies in another bank. How many pennies does he have in the two banks?

penny

[   ] _____
　　　label

2. Dee counted 79 flowers in the front garden. She counted 55 flowers in the back garden. How many flowers were there in all?

flowers

[   ] _____
　　　label

Add.

3.　72
　+ 49

4.　18
　+ 95

5.　56
　+ 38

6.　85
　+ 27

7.　79
　+ 56

8.　87
　+ 69

Homework

Use the diagram.

Square
Corners   4 Sides

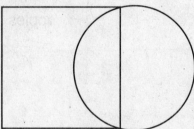

1. Draw a shape that belongs in each section of the diagram.

2. Draw a shape that belongs outside the diagram.

3. Explain why one of the shapes belongs where you put it.

_____

_____

_____

4. Jan writes 531 = 135. She says the numbers have the same value because 5 + 3 + 1 = 1 + 3 + 5.

   Bea says that Jan is wrong. Is Jan or Bea right? Explain your answer.

_____

_____

_____

Remembering

Solve each story problem.   **Show your work.**

1. Ms. Lee has 35 red apples and 47 green apples. How many apples does she have in all?

   [   ] _____
              label

apples

2. Pedro had 6 toy robots. His friend gave him more toy robots. Now he has 13 toy robots. How many toy robots did his friend give him?

   [   ] _____
              label

toy robots

3. Linda has 25 marbles. She got 16 more marbles. How many marbles does she have now?

   [   ] _____
              label

marbles

Add.

4.   97
   + 38

5.   53
   + 67

6.   76
   + 28

7. **Measurement** On a separate piece of paper, draw 3 shapes with the same perimeter.

Use Mathematical Processes

Name _____

Homework

Write the time in two different ways.

1.

_____ o'clock

2.

_____ o'clock

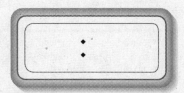

3.

_____ o'clock

Draw the hands on each analog clock and write the time on each digital clock below.

4.

1 o'clock

5.

6 o'clock

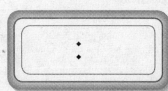

6.

12 o'clock

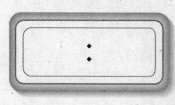

For each activity, ring the appropriate time.

7. Eat an afternoon snack.

    3:00 A.M.   2:00 P.M.   6:00 P.M.

8. Go to a movie at night.

    8:00 A.M.   12:00 NOON   7:00 P.M.

 9. On the Back Draw a picture of what you might do at 7:00 P.M. Draw a clock face with hands to show the time.

Name

Name _____

Homework

Write the time on the digital clocks.

1.

2.

3.

4.

Draw hands on the analog clocks to show the time.

5.

6.

7.

8.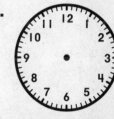

8:15 **11:20** **12:30** **1:45**

Fill in the answers.

9. 3 fives = _____

10. 7 fives = _____

11. 4 fives = _____

12. 8 fives = _____

13. 2 fives = _____

14. 5 fives = _____

15. 1 five = _____

16. 6 fives = _____

17. 9 fives = _____

 18. On the Back Draw a picture of what you were doing at 8:15 this morning. Draw an analog clock showing the time.

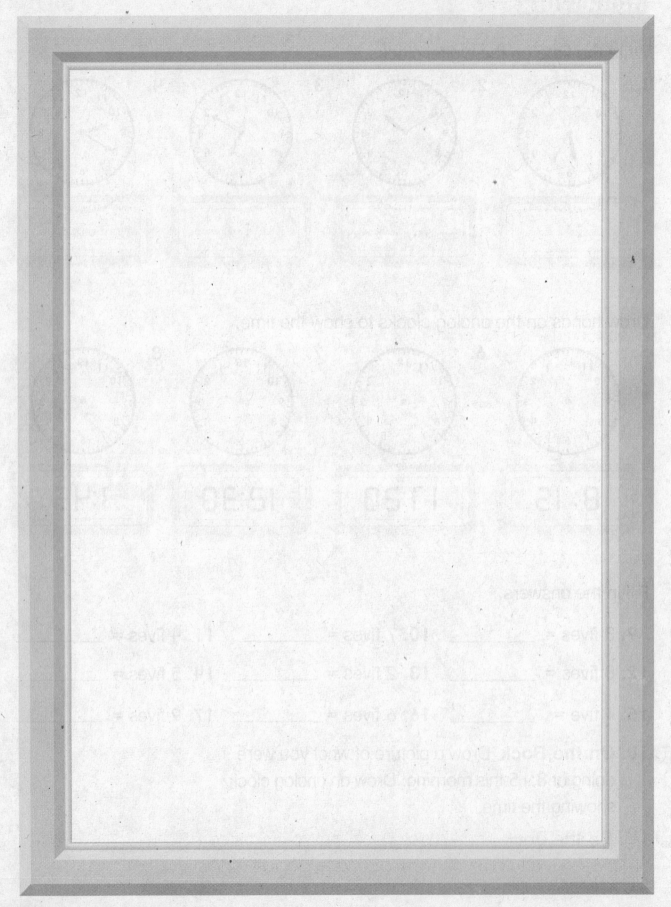

Name _____

Homework

Fill in the missing numbers on the clock faces below.
Draw hands on each clock to show the time.

1.    **2.**    **3.**    **4.**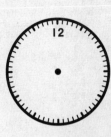

2:40   7:45   1:10   11:35

Write the time on each digital clock.

5.    **6.**    **7.**    **8.**

   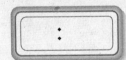      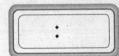

9. Write the time.

_____ minutes before _____

_____ minutes after _____

➡ **10. On the Back** Draw a picture of what you might do
at 7:15 A.M. and 7:15 P.M. Draw an analog clock showing
the time for each activity.

More on Telling Time

Name _____

Write the start and end times. Then find how much time passed.

Start Time	End Time	How Long Did It Take?
1.		
_____ P.M.	_____ P.M.	_____ hour(s)
2.		
_____ A.M.	_____ A.M.	_____ hour(s)
3.		
_____ A.M.	_____ A.M.	_____ hour(s)

For the activity, ring the unit of time you would use.

4. Bake cookies in an oven.

     days   seconds   minutes   months

5. On the Back Make a timetable showing how you spend the hours from the time you get home from school to the time you go to sleep.

Elapsed Time

Homework

Name _____

Use the calendar to answer questions 1 and 2.

January
S	M	T	W	TH	F	S
1	2	3	4	5	6	7
8	9	10	11	12	13	14
15	16	17	18	19	20	21
22	23	24	25	26	27	28
29	30	31				

February
S	M	T	W	TH	F	S
			1	2	3	4
5	6	7	8	9	10	11
12	13	14	15	16	17	18
19	20	21	22	23	24	25
26	27	28				

March
S	M	T	W	TH	F	S
			1	2	3	4
5	6	7	8	9	10	11
12	13	14	15	16	17	18
19	20	21	22	23	24	25
26	27	28	29	30	31	

April
S	M	T	W	TH	F	S
						1
2	3	4	5	6	7	8
9	10	11	12	13	14	15
16	17	18	19	20	21	22
23	24	25	26	27	28	29
30						

May
S	M	T	W	TH	F	S
	1	2	3	4	5	6
7	8	9	10	11	12	13
14	15	16	17	18	19	20
21	22	23	24	25	26	27
28	29	30	31			

June
S	M	T	W	TH	F	S
				1	2	3
4	5	6	7	8	9	10
11	12	13	14	15	16	17
18	19	20	21	22	23	24
25	26	27	28	29	30	

July
S	M	T	W	TH	F	S
						1
2	3	4	5	6	7	8
9	10	11	12	13	14	15
16	17	18	19	20	21	22
23	24	25	26	27	28	29
30	31					

August
S	M	T	W	TH	F	S
		1	2	3	4	5
6	7	8	9	10	11	12
13	14	15	16	17	18	19
20	21	22	23	24	25	26
27	28	29	30	31		

September
S	M	T	W	TH	F	S
					1	2
3	4	5	6	7	8	9
10	11	12	13	14	15	16
17	18	19	20	21	22	23
24	25	26	27	28	29	30

October
S	M	T	W	TH	F	S
1	2	3	4	5	6	7
8	9	10	11	12	13	14
15	16	17	18	19	20	21
22	23	24	25	26	27	28
29	30	31				

November
S	M	T	W	TH	F	S
			1	2	3	4
5	6	7	8	9	10	11
12	13	14	15	16	17	18
19	20	21	22	23	24	25
26	27	28	29	30		

December
S	M	T	W	TH	F	S
					1	2
3	4	5	6	7	8	9
10	11	12	13	14	15	16
17	18	19	20	21	22	23
24	25	26	27	28	29	30
31						

1. Which month immediately follows February?

_____

2. What day of the week does November begin with?

_____

Complete the table to solve the problem.

3. So Lum travels 8 miles each school day. How far does she travel in one school week?

_____ miles

Days	1	2	3	4	5
Distance (miles)					

4. On a separate piece of paper, write and solve your own problem using the calendar above.

Name _____

Remembering

Complete the table to solve each problem.

1. Samuel spends 4 hours practicing the piano every week. How many hours has he practiced after 5 weeks?

Weeks	1	2	3	4	5
Practice (hours)					

_____ hours

2. Marion spends 3 hours each day learning Mandarin Chinese. How many hours has she completed after 5 days?

Days	1	2	3	4	5
Practice (hours)					

_____ hours

Ring the most appropriate time.

3. Eat lunch.

7:00 A.M.   12:00 P.M.   5:00 P.M.

Ring the unit of time you would use.

4. Bake a cake in the oven.

seconds   minutes   hours   days

Calendars and Function Tables

Name _____

Use the picture graph to answer the questions.

Book Sales

Peter	▪	▪	▪	▪	▪					
Tammy	▪	▪	▪	▪						
Shana	▪	▪	▪	▪	▪	▪	▪	▪	▪	

1. Who sold the most books? _____

2. Who sold the fewest books? _____

3. How many more books did Shana sell than Tammy?

☐ _____
    label

4. How many fewer books did Peter sell than Shana?

☐ _____
    label

5. How many more books did Peter sell than Tammy?

☐ _____
    label

6. How many books did the children sell altogether?

☐ _____
    label

7. Write Your Own Write and solve your own question about the graph.

_____

_____

Targeted Practice

Use the picture graph to answer the questions.

Trucks Made in the Toy Shop

Misha	🚚	🚚	🚚	🚚	🚚	🚚				
Leroy	🚚	🚚	🚚	🚚	🚚	🚚	🚚	🚚	🚚	🚚
Ella	🚚	🚚	🚚	🚚	🚚	🚚	🚚			

I. Who made the most trucks? _____

2. Who made the fewest trucks? _____

3. How many more trucks did Leroy make than Misha?

☐ _____
       label

4. How many fewer trucks did Ella make than Leroy?

☐ _____
       label

5. How many more trucks did Ella make than Misha?

☐ _____
       label

6. How many trucks did the children make altogether?

☐ _____
       label

7. Write Your Own Write and solve your own question about the graph.

_____

_____

Compare to find how many **more** or **fewer**.
Write the number. Ring *more* or *fewer*.

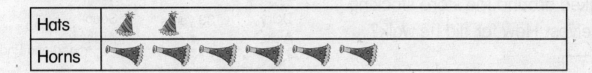

| Hats | |
| Horns | |

1. There are [   ] *more* *fewer* hats than horns.

2. There are [   ] *more* *fewer* horns than hats.

| Mina | |
| Emily | |

3. Mina has [   ] *more* *fewer* goldfish than Emily.

4. Emily has [   ] *more* *fewer* goldfish than Mina.

| Dan | |
| Tani | |

5. Dan has [   ] *more* *fewer* bells than Tani.

6. Tani has [   ] *more* *fewer* bells than Dan.

Remembering

Solve each story problem.

1. Here is the path Mr. Green took as he walked around the store stocking the shelves. How far did he walk?

   [   ] _____
            label

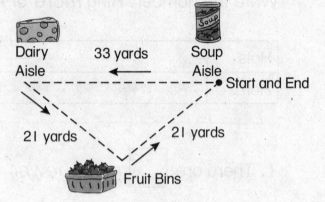

Dairy Aisle   33 yards   Soup Aisle
←   Start and End
21 yards   21 yards
Fruit Bins

2. Rose is helping to put a fence around her family's backyard. How much fencing should they buy?

   [   ] _____
            label

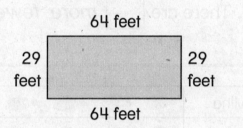

64 feet
29 feet   29 feet
64 feet

Add ones or tens. Make a Proof Drawing if it helps you.

3. $9 + 8 =$ _____
   $90 + 80 =$ _____

4. $7 + 7 =$ _____
   $70 + 70 =$ _____

5. $8 + 7 =$ _____
   $80 + 70 =$ _____

6. $6 + 5 =$ _____
   $60 + 50 =$ _____

---

7. Find the unknown partner.

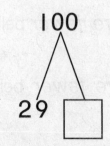

100
29 [   ]

       Read Picture Graphs

Homework

Compare. Ring the extra amount.
Write the number. Then ring *more* or *fewer*.

Pumpkins

Martin	🎃 🎃 🎃 🎃 🎃
Kerra	🎃 🎃 🎃 🎃 🎃 🎃 🎃

1. Martin has ☐ *more fewer* pumpkins than
   Kerra.

2. Kerra has ☐ *more fewer* pumpkins than
   Martin.

3. Martin needs ☐ pumpkins to have as many as
   Kerra.

4. Kerra must lose ☐ pumpkins to have as many as
   Martin.

Compare these numbers. Write the **is greater than** (>) or
is less than (<) sign in the circle. The first one is done for you.

5. 5 (<) 8   9 ◯ 3   6 ◯ 7

6. 1 ◯ 4   8 ◯ 6   4 ◯ 3

7. 6 ◯ 5   3 ◯ 7   9 ◯ 8

8. 5 ◯ 2   7 ◯ 9   1 ◯ 2

Targeted Practice

Compare. Ring the extra amount.
Write the number. Then ring *more* or *fewer*.

Peppers

Gina	🌶 🌶 🌶 🌶 🌶
Jesse	🌶 🌶 🌶 🌶 🌶 🌶 🌶 🌶

1. Gina has ☐ *more fewer* peppers than Jesse.

2. Jesse has ☐ *more fewer* peppers than Gina.

3. Gina needs ☐ peppers to have as many as Jesse.

4. Jesse must give away ☐ peppers to have as many as Gina.

Bears

Marco	🐻 🐻 🐻 🐻 🐻 🐻 🐻
Alena	🐻 🐻 🐻 🐻 🐻 🐻 🐻 🐻 🐻

5. Marco has ☐ *more fewer* bears than Alena.

6. Alena has ☐ *more fewer* bears than Marco.

7. Marco needs ☐ bears to have as many as Alena.

8. Alena must give away ☐ bears to have as many as Marco.

The Language of Comparison

Homework

Solve each story problem.   **Show your work.**

1. Yesterday, Annie saw 17 ducks at the park. Cristina saw 8 ducks. How many more ducks did Annie see than Cristina?

   ☐ _____
   label

2. Juan made 6 fruit cups for the picnic this afternoon. Teresa made 9 more fruit cups than Juan. How many fruit cups did Teresa make?

   ☐ _____
   label

3. Michelle collected 13 baseballs. Rini collected 7 baseballs. How many more baseballs does Rini have to collect to have as many baseballs as Michelle?

   ☐ _____
   label

4. Tom has 12 horses on his farm. He has 4 fewer chickens than horses. How many chickens does Tom have?

   ☐ _____
   label

Name _____

Remembering

Solve each story problem.   **Show your work.**

1. Mr. Gomez has 75 cans of beans. Each shelf
   holds 10 cans. How many shelves can he fill with
   cans of beans? How many cans will be left over?

   [ ] shelves   [ ] cans left over

2. Abigail has 39 stamps in her collection. She puts
   10 stamps on each page of her stamp book.
   How many pages can she fill with stamps? How
   many stamps will be left over?

   [ ] pages   [ ] stamps left over

Add.

3. $45 + 8 =$ _____ $22 + 4 =$ _____ $86 + 3 =$ _____

Add.

4. $60 + 20 =$ _____ $90 + 80 =$ _____ $70 + 30 =$ _____

   $6 + 2 =$ _____ $9 + 8 =$ _____ $7 + 3 =$ _____

5. $50 + 70 =$ _____ $40 + 90 =$ _____ $20 + 40 =$ _____

   $5 + 7 =$ _____ $4 + 9 =$ _____ $2 + 4 =$ _____

6. Find the unknown partner.

100

[ ]   54

         Pose and Solve Comparison Story Problems

Homework

Use the table. Fill in the boxes with numbers.
Ring *more* or *fewer*.

	Toys	Games
Jake	5	9
Kara	8	4

1. Jake has ☐ *more fewer* games than Kara.

2. Kara has ☐ *more fewer* games than Jake.

3. Kara has ☐ *more fewer* toys than Jake.

4. Jake has ☐ *more fewer* toys than Kara.

5. The children have ☐ games altogether.

6. The children have ☐ toys altogether.

7. Kara must give away ☐ toys to have as many as Jake.

8. Kara must get ☐ games to have as many as Jake.

Targeted Practice

Use the table. Fill in the boxes with numbers.
Ring *more* or *fewer*.

	Books	CDs
Meg	7	2
Kate	9	5
Andrew	3	8

1. Kate has ☐ *more fewer* CDs than Andrew.

2. Meg has ☐ *more fewer* books than Kate.

3. Andrew has ☐ *more fewer* CDs than Kate.

4. The children have ☐ books altogether.

5. Meg needs ☐ books to have as many as Kate.

6. Andrew must get ☐ books to have as many as Meg.

7. Meg must get ☐ CDs to have as many as Andrew.

8. Kate and Andrew have a total of ☐ CDs.

Tables

Homework

Chen has 7 markers. Linda has 4 markers.

1. Make a table to show this.

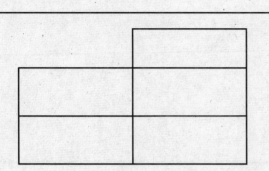

2. Turn the table into a picture graph.

Use a circle for each 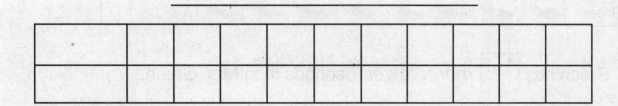.

Compare. Circle the extra amount in the graph above.
Write the number. Then ring *more* or *fewer* below.

3. Linda has ⬚ *more fewer* markers than Chen.

4. Chen has ⬚ *more fewer* markers than Linda.

5. Linda needs ⬚ markers to have as many as Chen.

6. Chen must lose ⬚ markers to have as many as Linda.

Name _____

Remembering

Solve the story problem.   **Show your work.**

1. Mrs. Green put away 63 bags of
   peanuts. Mr. Green put away 58
   bags of peanuts. How many bags of
   peanuts did they put away in all?

   [ ] _____
                label

Compare. Ring the extra amount.
Write the number. Then ring *more* or *fewer*.

| Mr. Green | 🫛 🫛 🫛 🫛 |
| Mrs. Green | 🫛 🫛 🫛 🫛 🫛 🫛 🫛 🫛 |

2. Mr. Green has [ ] *more fewer* peapods than Mrs. Green.

3. Mr. Green needs [ ] peapods to have as many as Mrs. Green.

Compare. Write the **is greater than** (>) or
is less than (<) sign in the circle.

4. 3 ◯ 9   8 ◯ 6   4 ◯ 2

5. 7 ◯ 1   2 ◯ 4   6 ◯ 5

---

6. Find the unknown partner.   100

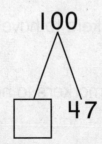

Convert Tables to Picture Graphs

Name _____

Homework

1. Prince won 8 medals at the dog show. Lady won
   5 medals. Muffy won 3 medals. Make a table to
   show this.

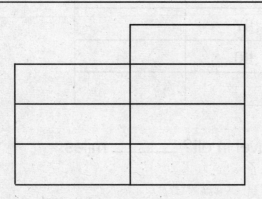

2. Turn the table into a picture graph. Use a circle for
   each 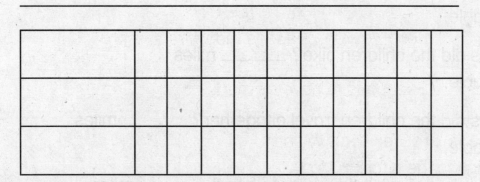.

Compare. Write the number. Ring _more_ or _fewer._

3. Prince has [   ] _more fewer_ medals than Muffy.

4. Muffy has [   ] _more fewer_ medals than Prince.

5. Lady needs [   ] medals to have as many as Prince.

6. Lady must lose [   ] medals to have as many as Muffy.

Name _____

Targeted Practice

Beth and Hamal like to go hiking and biking.
The table shows how many miles the children traveled.

Number of Miles Traveled

	Hiking	Biking	Total
Beth	19	47	
Hamal	36	48	
Total			

1. How many miles did Hamal travel in all? _____ miles
   Put this in the table.

2. How many miles did Beth travel in all? _____ miles
   Put this in the table.

3. How many miles did the children hike? _____ miles
   Put this in the table.

4. How many miles did the children bike? _____ miles
   Put this in the table.

5. How many miles did the children travel altogether? _____ miles
   Put this in the table.

6. Find the total number of miles the children hiked. _____ miles

   The partners are _____ and _____.

7. Find the total number of miles the children biked. _____ miles

   The partners are _____ and _____.

8. Find the total number of miles Beth traveled. _____ miles

   The partners are _____ and _____.

9. Find the total number of miles Hamal traveled. _____ miles

   The partners are _____ and _____.

Graph Data

Homework

1. The park has 9 oak trees, 2 maple trees, and 6 elm trees in it. Complete the table to show this.

Trees in the Park

Oak	
Maple	
Elm	

2. Use the data table to complete the bar graph.

Trees in the Park

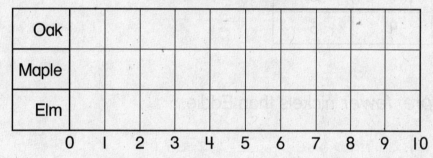

Use your bar graph. Fill in the missing number and ring *more* or *fewer*.

3. There are ☐ *more   fewer* oak trees than maple trees in the park.

4. There are ☐ *more   fewer* maple trees than elm trees in the park.

5. We need to plant ☐ *more   fewer* elm trees to have as many elm trees as oak trees.

Remembering

1. Write the total amount of money.

     _____

Use the table to answer the questions. Fill in the boxes
with the numbers. Ring *more* or *fewer* if you need to.

	Nickels	Dimes
Jessica	7	3
Eddie	4	5

2. Jessica has ☐ *more fewer* nickels than Eddie.

3. Eddie has ☐ *more fewer* nickels than Jessica.

4. Eddie must give away ☐ dimes to have as many
dimes as Jessica.

Add.

5. 100 + 96 = _____   62 + 100 = _____   100 + 7 = _____

10 + 96 = _____   62 + 10 = _____   10 + 7 = _____

1 + 96 = _____   62 + 1 = _____   1 + 7 = _____

Introduce Bar Graphs

Homework

Use the bar graph to complete the sentences.
Ring *more* or *fewer*.

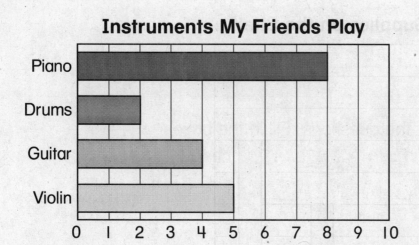

Instruments My Friends Play

1. ☐ *more fewer* children play the drums than the guitar.

2. ☐ *more fewer* children play the drums than the violin.

3. ☐ *more fewer* children play the piano than the drums.

4. ☐ *more fewer* children play the piano than the guitar.

5. ☐ *more fewer* children play the violin than the piano.

6. ☐ children play the piano or the drums.

7. ☐ children play the piano, guitar, and violin altogether.

Name _____

Targeted Practice

Use the bar graph to complete the sentences.
Ring *more* or *fewer.*

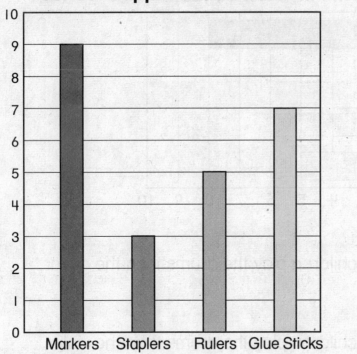

School Supplies on the Shelf

Markers   Staplers   Rulers   Glue Sticks

1. There are [ ] *more fewer* markers on the shelf than rulers.

2. There are [ ] *more fewer* staplers on the shelf than glue sticks.

3. There are [ ] *more fewer* markers on the shelf than staplers.

4. There are [ ] *more fewer* glue sticks on the shelf than rulers.

5. There are [ ] *more fewer* rulers on the shelf than staplers.

6. There are *more fewer* markers than there are rulers and staplers combined.

7. There is a total of [ ] glue sticks and markers.

Read Bar Graphs

Homework

Use the bar graph to answer the questions below.
Fill in the circle next to the correct answer.

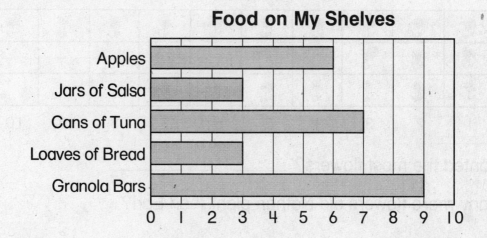

Food on My Shelves

1. How many more cans of tuna are there than jars of salsa?

   ○ 4
   ○ 5
   ○ 6
   ○ 7

2. Altogether, how many apples and granola bars do I have?

   ○ 11
   ○ 13
   ○ 15
   ○ 16

3. I have the same number of which two foods?

   ○ Apples and granola bars
   ○ Apples and tuna
   ○ Salsa and bread
   ○ Tuna and granola bars

4. **Write Your Own** Write 1 question about the graph. Answer your question.

_____

_____

Name _____

Remembering

Use the picture graph to answer the questions.

Flowers Planted in the Garden

	1	2	3	4	5	6	7	8	9	10
Tuti	🌷	🌷	🌷	🌷	🌷	🌷	🌷	🌷	🌷	🌷
Earl	🌷	🌷	🌷							
Nathan	🌷	🌷	🌷	🌷	🌷	🌷	🌷			

1. Who planted the most flowers? _____

2. How many more flowers did Nathan plant than Earl?

   ☐ _____

   label

3. How many fewer flowers did Earl plant than Tuti?

   ☐ _____

   label

Add. Make a Proof Drawing if it helps.

4. $\begin{array}{r} 76 \\ + 39 \\ \hline \end{array}$ $\begin{array}{r} 43 \\ + 78 \\ \hline \end{array}$ $\begin{array}{r} 52 \\ + 87 \\ \hline \end{array}$

5. $\begin{array}{r} 61 \\ + 75 \\ \hline \end{array}$ $\begin{array}{r} 57 \\ + 98 \\ \hline \end{array}$ $\begin{array}{r} 89 \\ + 48 \\ \hline \end{array}$

6. Find the unknown partner.

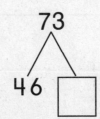

Analyze Information in Bar Graphs

Name _____

Homework

Use the information in the circle graph to answer the questions below. Fill in the circle next to the correct answer.

Toys in the Playroom

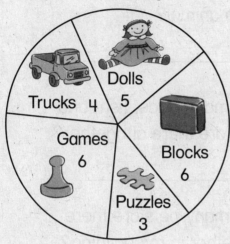

1. The teacher told Brandie to bring her all of the dolls and games. How many toys does Brandie have to bring to the teacher?

   ○ 9
   ○ 10
   ○ 11
   ○ 12

2. How many more blocks are there than trucks?

   ○ 1
   ○ 2
   ○ 4
   ○ 6

3. The playroom has the same number of which two kinds of toys?

   ○ blocks and dolls
   ○ dolls and puzzles
   ○ games and blocks
   ○ trucks and puzzles

4. There is 1 fewer truck than _____.

   ○ blocks
   ○ dolls
   ○ games
   ○ puzzles

5. There are 3 more games than _____.

   ○ blocks
   ○ dolls
   ○ puzzles
   ○ trucks

Targeted Practice

Use the information in the circle graph to answer
the questions.

Pets in My Building

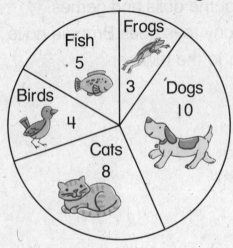

1. My building has the most of
which animal?

_____

2. How many birds, fish, and
frogs are there altogether?

_____

3. How many pets are there
altogether in my building?

_____

4. How many more dogs are
there than frogs?

_____

5. How many fewer fish are
there than cats?

_____

Use the information in the circle graph to complete each
sentence.

6. There is 1 fewer bird than
there are _____.

7. There are 3 more cats than
there are _____.

8. There is 1 more bird than
there are _____.

9. There are 2 fewer cats than
there are _____.

Introduce Circle Graphs

Homework

Use the information in the circle graph to answer the questions below. Fill in the circle next to the correct answer.

Toys in the Box

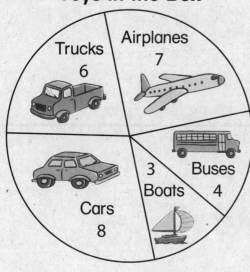

Trucks 6 · Airplanes 7 · Cars 8 · Boats 3 · Buses 4

1. There is 1 fewer truck than there are _____.
- ○ airplanes
- ○ boats
- ○ buses
- ○ cars

2. There are 2 more trucks than there are _____.
- ○ airplanes
- ○ boats
- ○ buses
- ○ cars

3. There are 5 fewer boats than there are _____.
- ○ airplanes
- ○ boats
- ○ cars
- ○ trucks

4. How many cars, boats, and airplanes are there in the box?
- ○ 17
- ○ 18
- ○ 20
- ○ 28

5. What is the total number of buses and trucks in the box?
- ○ 4
- ○ 8
- ○ 10
- ○ 12

Remembering

Solve each story problem.

Show your work.

1. Erin has 14 shirts in her closet. Vana has 6 shirts in her closet. How many more shirts does Erin have than Vana?

☐ _____
　　　label

2. 17 people went to Hoon's party. 9 people went to Mark's party. How many fewer people were at Mark's party than Hoon's?

☐ _____
　　　label

Is the answer correct?
Write *yes* or *no*. If *no*, fix the exercise.

3.　　 37　OK?
　　 + 65　☐
　　 ─────
　　　102

4.　　 57　OK?
　　 + 26　☐
　　 ─────
　　　 73

5.　　 42　OK?
　　 + 59　☐
　　 ─────
　　　911

6.　　 17　OK?
　　 + 45　☐
　　 ─────
　　　 71

7.　　 69　OK?
　　 + 13　☐
　　 ─────
　　　 72

8.　　 51　OK?
　　 + 35　☐
　　 ─────
　　　 86

9. Find the unknown partner.

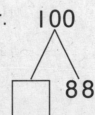

100

☐　88

Explore Circle Graphs

Homework

Name _____

1. Complete the horizontal bar graph using
   the information given below.

   - Jun has 5 marbles.

   - Angela has 3 more marbles than Jun.

   - Janell has to lose 4 marbles to have
     as many as Jun.

   - Caroline has 2 fewer marbles than Angela.

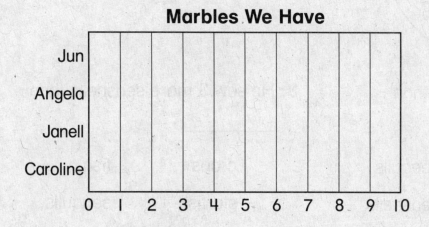

Marbles We Have

Compare the numbers below. Use **is greater than** (>) or
is less than (<). The first one is done for you.

2. 6 $<$ 9   7 ◯ 4   2 ◯ 3

3. 8 ◯ 5   1 ◯ 10   4 ◯ 1

4. 6 ◯ 0   8 ◯ 3   7 ◯ 8

Remembering

Use the information in the circle graph to answer the
questions below. Fill in the circle next to the correct answer.

What Jared Saw at the Beach

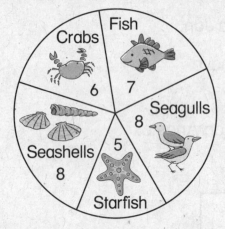

1. How many more seagulls did
   Jared see than fish?

   ○ 1 more   ○ 4 more

   ○ 2 more   ○ 5 more

2. He saw 1 fewer crab than

   _____ .

   ○ starfish   ○ seagulls

   ○ fish   ○ seashells

3. He saw 3 more seashells than

   _____ .

   ○ crabs   ○ fish

   ○ starfish   ○ seagulls

Complete the number sequence. Write the rule.

4. 12, 20, 28, _____, _____, _____   Rule: *n* _____

5. 38, 41, 44, _____, _____, _____   Rule: *n* _____

6. 93, 88, 83, _____, _____, _____   Rule: *n* _____

7. Find the unknown partner.

68

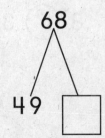

49

Homework

Lena and Paulo test light bulbs. The table shows what they found. Answer each question and fill in the table with your answers.

Working Light Bulbs

	Green	Yellow	Total
Paulo	47	51	
Lena	38	29	
Total			

1. How many green bulbs worked? _____ green bulbs

2. How many of Paulo's bulbs worked? _____ bulbs

3. How many of Lena's bulbs worked? _____ bulbs

4. How many bulbs worked in total? _____ bulbs

Use the bar graph to answer the questions.

Bike Trails (in miles)

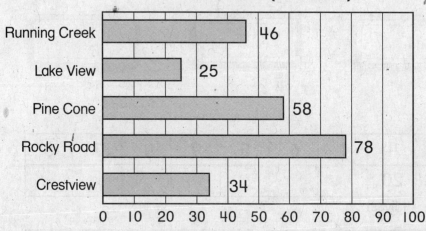

5. A bike race is held on Pine Cone and Lake View trails. How long is the race?

   _____ miles

6. You want to ride exactly 80 miles this week. Which two trails should you take?

   _____ and

   _____

7. How far will you go if you ride Pine Cone and Rocky Road?

   _____ miles

2-Digit Addition with Tables and Graphs **165**

Remembering

Draw the hands on the clock to show the time.

1.

| 5:30 | 11:15 | 6:50 | 12:00 |

Write the time on the digital clock.

2.

 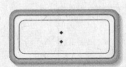  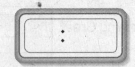

Complete the tables.

3.

Big hand points to	4	I	6	5	9	4	7	8
Time in minutes	20							

(4 fives)

4.

Big hand points to	8	II	10	6	9	7	5	3
Time in minutes	40							

(8 fives)

5. Find the unknown partner.

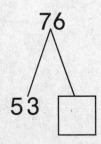

76

53

2-Digit Addition with Tables and Graphs

Name _____

Homework

Answer the questions about the data.

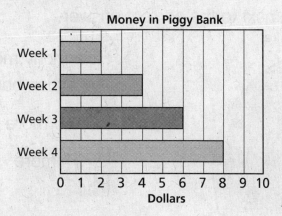

Money in Piggy Bank

1. How many dollars were in the bank in
   Week 1? _____ in Week 2? _____ in
   Week 3? _____ in Week 4? _____

2. What pattern do you see?

   _____

   _____

3. What do you predict will happen in Week 5?

   _____

Collect and record data by tossing a dime.
Answer the questions.

Turn	1	2	3	4	5	6	7	8	9	10
Toss										

4. Fill in the table. Use H for heads and T for Tails.

   _____

5. Do you see a pattern?

   _____

   _____

6. Can you accurately predict what will happen
   with the next turn? Explain.

   _____

Name _____

Remembering

Use the information in the circle graph to answer the questions below. Fill in the circle next to the correct answer.

Fruit in the Basket

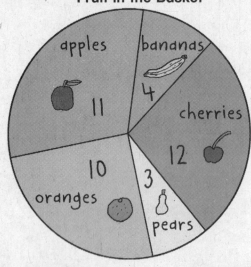

1. How many more oranges are there than bananas?

   ◯ 14 more   ◯ 6 more

   ◯ 7 more   ◯ 5 more

2. There is 1 fewer apple than

   _____ .

   ◯ oranges   ◯ bananas

   ◯ cherries   ◯ pears

3. There are 8 more apples than

   _____ .

   ◯ oranges   ◯ bananas

   ◯ cherries   ◯ pears

Complete the number sequence. Write the rule.

4. 14, 20, 26, _____, _____, _____   Rule: n _____

5. 78, 80, 82, _____, _____, _____   Rule: n _____

6. 93, 83, 73, _____, _____, _____   Rule: n _____

7. Find the unknown partner.

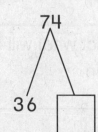

Homework

1. Draw 3 rectangles each with a perimeter of 24 units. Label the length and width.

2. Choose one rectangle. Write directions for drawing the rectangle.

   _____

   _____

   _____

   _____

   _____

3. Predict how many times you can fold a piece of paper in half.

   _____

4. Try it. How many times did you fold the paper in half?

   _____

5. Why did you have to stop folding?

   _____

   _____

Name _____

Remembering

Draw the hands on the clock to show the time.

1.

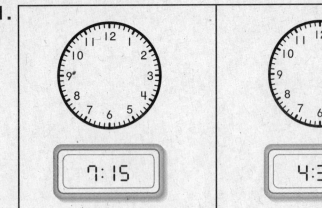

| 7:15 | 4:30 | 2:00 |

Write the time on the digital clock.

2.

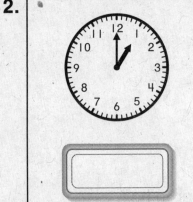 

Complete the number sequence. Write the rule.

3. 10, 16, 22, _____, _____, _____   Rule: *n* _____

4. 65, 67, 69, _____, _____, _____   Rule: *n* _____

5. 74, 71, 68, _____, _____, _____   Rule: *n* _____

Use Mathematical Processes